THE NAKED WALL

THE NAKED WALL

Inspiring Ideas for Paint, Unique Finishes, Wall Coverings, and Art

BOLD-PRYOR & DONNA V. LACIS

WATSON-GUPTILL PUBLICATIONS / NEW YORK

Senior Acquisitions Editor: Victoria Craven
Project Editor: Martha Moran
Designer: Barbara Balch
Production Manager: Hector Campbell

First published in 2006 by Watson-Guptill Publications,
a division of VNU Business Media, Inc.
770 Broadway, New York, N.Y. 10003
www.wgpub.com

Library of Congress Cataloging-in-Publication Data

Bold-Pryor, Anne.
  The naked wall.
     p. cm.
  Text by Anne Bold-Pryor and Donna V. Lacis.
  Includes bibliographical references and index.
  ISBN 0-8230-3152-7 (alk. paper)
  1. Wall coverings. 2. Texture painting. 3. Wall hangings. 4. Interior decoration. I. Lacis,
Donna V. II. Title.
  NK2115.5.W3B65 2006
  747'.3--dc22
                          2005029915

Manufactured in Hong Kong

First printing, 2006

1 2 3 4 5 6 7 8 9 / 14 13 12 11 10 09 08 07 06

ACKNOWLEDGMENTS

We offer many, many thanks to our families, friends, and clients (our newest
friends) for opening their hearts and homes to us throughout the process of creating our book. Thank you to Virginia Trevino for sewing many of the beautiful window treatments; Frank Collins for the fine workmanship in reupholstering all those
sofas and chairs; Sam Stone-Street for his endless hours of repainting all those
builder beige rooms; and David Stevens for all the wonderful advice on anything
wallpaper. We would be remiss without thanking Pam O'Brien and Drew Matoske
for their creative and technical expertise in helping us develop the interactive CD,
which ultimately led to our relationship with Watson-Guptill. And also, thanks to
Will Bloodworth of Alpenglow Imaging for his plethora of knowledge and his
expertise in everything regarding digital photography.

    And finally, to Victoria Craven, our senior editor, for believing in our book
from the very beginning; Martha Moran, our editor, for her painstaking guidance
throughout the creative process, as well as for her inspired way with words; and
Barbara Balch, our designer, for making the pages come to life.

747.3
BOLD

For Edmunds

—*D.V.L.*

For John, Max, and Ben

—*A.B-P.*

CONTENTS

PART I: DRESS IT 10

PART II: ACCESSORIZE IT 104

A NOTE FROM THE AUTHORS

This book, a dream of ours for a long time, is now a reality. Though neither of us is professionally trained in the field of interior design, we each have a strong passion and interest in it dating back to our childhoods. Until we met almost ten years ago, most of our design work had been done in our own homes and those of friends and family. Then we had the good fortune to meet each other, literally over a Crate and Barrel shopping bag in Hong Kong, and a wonderfully fulfilling design partnership (and friendship) began. Anne soon landed us our first notable client and our relationship took off from there. We have been inseparable ever since, even now that we live half a world away from each other.

Over the years, we have collaborated on a variety of interior design projects in Hong Kong and throughout the United States and we've learned something new and unique from each experience. We have explored and shopped various parts of the world, always searching for the next great idea. We have also collaborated on other projects that all somehow relate to the home—from designing and marketing home accessories, to writing and producing home-design television news inserts, to writing a monthly newspaper column on home décor. We never stop looking and learning, whatever the endeavor. In *The Naked Wall,* we share what we have learned and reinvented along the way.

This book is meant to be fun as well as inspirational, because fun is what we have when we tackle a project together. So, be creative and step out of the beige box! Remember, it's only paint and a few holes in the wall. And honestly, sharing the work with a friend makes it all the more fulfilling. We speak from experience.

Anne & Donna

INTRODUCTION

A couple of years ago, we decided to take on a new challenge and write a book to share our home decorating ideas and experiences. Our concept was quite simple: show how a home can be transformed from blah to ahhh with a minimal investment of time and money. Decorating or designing a room can be a daunting and overwhelming experience. Where do you start: with a paint color? a piece of fabric? a favorite oil painting? What exactly is a naked wall? Does it need paint, wallpaper, or, a faux finish? Is it missing artwork, accessories, or a special family heirloom?

The Naked Wall is a guided tour of the process of decorating your naked walls from beginning (color ideas and inspirations) to end (displaying art and collections). We'll tell you how to make choices and decisions, where to find inspiration and ideas, and how to create an environment with impact, one that reflects your tastes, style, and personality.

Though not a traditional "how-to" book, we do tell you how to achieve diverse looks and effects, and how to execute various techniques and projects, in clear easy-to-follow instructions, including lists of the materials and supplies you'll need. (A detailed *Materials and Supplies Glossary* begins on page 174.) We offer some personal anecdotes which we hope will provide insight and tips and ideas to make your naked wall experiences easier to tackle and more rewarding.

Please don't get discouraged when you make mistakes (even the pros make them). Decorating your home is an ongoing learning process and you'll often find that your mistakes lead you to even better results than what you originally envisioned. And, don't worry, we let you know what projects are better left to the professionals.

Note: Great care has been taken to faithfully reproduce the paint chip colors in this book. Because color reproduction is not always absolutely accurate, there may be subtle variations between the paint chip colors reproduced here and the actual paint chips.

PART I: DRESS IT

The Painted Wall • The Papered Wall • The Other Wall

Japanese woven wallpaper was installed on just one wall to highlight the pair of Chinese tapered cabinets.

CHAPTER I

THE PAINTED WALL

What is the quickest and simplest way to give the appearance of a total room makeover? The answer is simple: change the paint color. It is easy, inexpensive, and requires a small investment of time and money in exchange for a big return and instant gratification.

Benjamin Moore
Potpourri Green
2029-50

Opposite: The neutral furnishings, flooring, and trim pop off the walls, painted Benjamin Moore Potpourri Green. The color reflects the homeowners' zest for life. The banana leaf dining chairs add color and texture to the simple, yet graceful, dining area.

Above: The Potpourri Green walls accentuate the clean lines and neutral upholstery of the Barbara Barry for Baker armless chairs.

CHOOSING COLOR

Choosing the perfect paint color is tricky. It has taken us years of practice to be able to make the right color choices. And even with practice, we sometimes have had to repaint a room a second time. It's not easy to envision an entire room using the little paint chips from the hardware store, but here's how to make it easier.

THE COLOR WHEEL

Before we explore ways to select the perfect color for your room, let's look at colors and how they relate to one another. The obvious starting point is the color wheel. It is made-up of the primary colors: red, yellow, and blue; and, the secondary colors (one primary color mixed with another primary): orange, green, and violet (red and yellow make orange; blue and yellow make green; and red and blue make violet.) Without getting too technical and detailed, there are also tertiary colors (a primary color combined with its adjacent secondary color): red combined with orange, its adjacent secondary color, produces the tertiary color red-orange; red combined with its other adjacent secondary color, violet, produces the tertiary color red-violet.

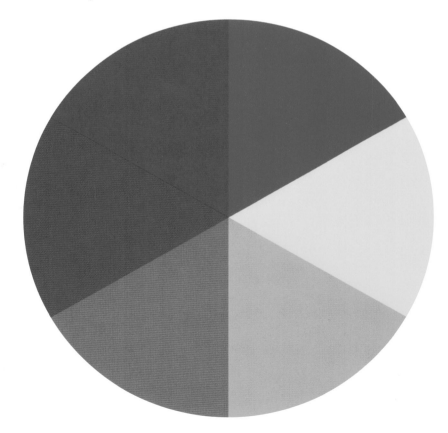

WARM AND COOL COLORS

Beyond the color wheel, colors can also be categorized into two distinct groups: warm and cool. Reds, oranges, and yellows are warm colors, while greens, blues, and violets are cool. This is not to say you can't achieve warmth in rooms with cool colors, or a cool, calm feeling in rooms with warm colors.

Left: The burnt orange walls enhance the warmth of this English country kitchen.

Above: The cool greenish khaki wall color is an unexpected, yet beautiful choice for this traditional setting.

COLOR TINTS AND SHADES

A tint of a color is made by adding white to it and a shade of a color is made by adding black. The use of one color and its various tints and shades creates a monochromatic color scheme, which can make a space feel larger and more unified. The opposite approach, a complementary color scheme, uses colors found opposite each other on the color wheel, which makes each color seem stronger and more vivid.

Now that we've given you traditional color theory in a nutshell, don't ever be afraid to mix things up! We often do, and love the results.

Below: The monochromatic color scheme of soft greens creates a quiet sanctuary in this master bedroom.

Behr Harvest Brown 710D-4

Above: Behr Harvest Brown was used as a subtle backdrop for this living room, entrance hall, and staircase. The combination of soft taupe tones in this monochromatic color scheme brings a sense of comort and tranquility to the space.

HOW COLOR AFFECTS
SPACE AND MOOD

The mood and environment that you want to create should be a factor in making your color choices. Do you want a formal or informal room? Do you want to relax and feel calm in the room, or enhance lively conversation? The room's function is another important consideration when choosing color. Is it a children's or an adult's room? Will there be lots of traffic and wear and tear, or occasional use? Painting a media room a very dark color will enhance movie viewing. Cooler colors often work better in rooms where relaxing and unwinding is the goal, such as a bedroom or reading room. Warmer colors tend to work better in rooms where social activities occur, like a kitchen or family room.

Behr Dry Sea Grass 360-F-4

The open living and dining room combination was painted using Behr Dry Sea Grass, a color inspired by a shade in the Heriz Persian carpet. The glass coffee table allows the beauty of the carpet to shine through.

Above: This beautiful French Country style living room, painted a pale yellow, is decorated with all of Missy's favorite things: flowers, animal prints, and toiles.

Opposite: A living room painted a classic creamy beige is ideal for the soft furnishings and flea market finds. The painting was given to Nancy by her grandmother and is one of her favorite pieces.

AFFECTS ON COLOR

Location is another factor to consider when selecting a paint color. The same color can look entirely different on the four walls within a room, depending on lighting and the time of day. Take into account the direction the room is facing; rooms facing west will receive bright afternoon sunlight, rooms facing east get softer, morning light.

The furniture and design elements of the room are also important. White kitchen cabinets will reflect more of the true wall color than wooden cabinets. Different tones and types of wood affect the wall color in different ways. The color you choose can blend with those tones or it can play off them and highlight the wood color or finish.

Do It:
Testing Color Options

We always, always, always test paint colors prior to painting an entire room.

You can test directly on the wall, or on sample boards. Either way, be sure the test area is at least 12" x 12" and that you test on each wall that will be painted. Look at the test colors at various times of the day and night and with different lighting options. Be sure to use the actual wall primer in your tests and apply as many coats of primer and paint color as you will to the wall.

Difficulty Factor: Beginner
Time Factor: Minutes
Materials and Supplies:
2"–4" throwaway paint-brushes
Paint and primer
Sample board

Benjamin Moore and Ralph Lauren offer two-ounce sample colors that we absolutely love. They allow you to test many different paint colors without breaking the bank. However, they don't stock their entire paint collection in this size. If the paint you want isn't available in a sample size, purchase a quart. You may end up making several trips to the paint store for additional sample colors, but it's worth taking a bit more time in the test stage to guarantee you've got the right color when you paint the entire room.

TYPES OF PAINT

There are four different paint finishes that we typically use: flat, eggshell, semi-gloss, and high-gloss. Flat paint is forgiving and hides many wall imperfections, but it shows wear and tear and is best used in rooms where fingerprints are not a consideration. High-gloss and semi-gloss paints are great for high traffic areas and trims because they are washable. Most of the time, we use an eggshell finish, which combines some of the advantages of both flat and gloss finishes—it hides imperfections and can be cleaned. Each manufacturer has its own paint finish variations and terminology.

. . . .

Design Diary:
Matching Paint Color

My son Max wanted a new look for his bedroom. He thought the walls would look great painted the same color as his beloved away soccer jersey and he quickly found an exact color match on my paint wheel. I explained that although this chip was the exact color of his jersey, when on the walls it would actually look much brighter. I suggested an alternate, deeper shades of the color, but, being the stubborn 11 year old that he was, we went with his original choice. After the first wall was painted, Max wanted to know why the color looked funny—it was too light and too bright. We ended up repainting the room in a deeper shade of the original color; it matched the soccer jersey perfectly. Now, whenever Max questions my advice, I reply, "Remember the blue paint chip?"

Anne

*Lowe's Rolling Sea
5001-10B*
Original choice:
color of jersey

*Lowe's La Fonda
Deep Blue Sea
4011-7*
The final wall color

COLOR INSPIRATION

nspiration for wall color can come from anywhere: a flower in your garden, a pair of shoes, a tie, even the family pet. Consider how your color choice will work with existing furniture, bedding, upholstery, flooring, window treatments, etc. This is called "backing into a color." If you're starting from scratch, wall color shouldn't be the first decision you make. Rather, select the new sofa or new rug, and then work your way towards a paint color. It is much easier to find a paint color to go with new furnishings than the other way around.

Opposite: The deep tones of the furnishings and wood floor inspired the use of Benjamin Moore Greenbrier Beige in a washable eggshell finish in the entrance foyer and the hallways in this home.

Left: Buttery walls provide an inviting environment for the antique New Mexican rugs. The tonal raw silk drapes act as a headboard and perfectly complement the mixture of textiles used for the bedding.

Benjamin Moore
Greenbrier Beige
HC-79

BACKING INTO A COLOR

Look at the objects in your room for inspiration: rugs, upholstery, window treatments, accessories, and artwork will provide good clues to the perfect color choice. Perhaps your sofa, rug, drapes, and favorite vase all contain a similar shade of green. If you select a tint or shade of this same green for your wall color, a monochromatic approach, the atmosphere in the room will veer towards serene. But if you choose a complementary color for the walls, in this case that would be red, the room will be more lively and energetic. The wall color does not have to match other colors in the room—it can merely be in the same color family or just complement the existing colors.

Above: The vibrant red walls provide the perfect backdrop for the neutral tones of the upholstery and draperies in the elegant, formal living and dining rooms.

Opposite: The pumpkin-colored chair and ottoman, upholstered in Nina Campbell's Indore Stripe Chenille, add a splash of rich color to the otherwise tranquil living room. Small accents of pumpkin and cognac are mixed throughout the room, which was painted using Pittsburgh Paint Linen White.

COLOR IMPACT

Wall color can have a huge impact and is one of the key ingredients for influencing the overall look of the room. Color impact can come from other sources in a room, too. An empty room with neutral, off-white walls has low, or no, color impact. But when a fabulous upholstered sofa, a contemporary coffee table, or stunning art is introduced, the off-white walls provide the perfect backdrop for color impact. Alternatively, black or red walls create dramatic impact in a room full of neutral furnishings and accessories. When it comes to color impact, it all depends on where you want the impact to come from!

Benjamin Moore
G.I. Green
2149-20

Design Diary:
Choosing Color

Anne's newlywed sister, Patty, and her husband Chris, were having a difficult time choosing a paint color for their bedroom. One day, at nearly the exact same moment, they each spotted a man wearing an intense army green t-shirt. They looked at each other and knew it was the perfect compromise for their new bedroom. As it turned out, the actual color that went up on the wall was Benjamin Moore G.I. Green!

Donna

Left: The creamy beige walls provide the neutral background for the colors in the upholstery, the window treatments, and the accessories.

The crisp white painted walls are the perfect backdrop for the two sectional sofas in the open great room which were placed to mirror each other. The upholstered pieces are from Ligne Roset.

The contemporary style of the entire home dictated the white wall color throughout. The stainless steel stools, Precision Stool with Backrest from Design Within Reach, were the perfect choice to complete the kitchen. The dining chairs are from Ligne Roset.

NEUTRALS

There is a reason the classic neutrals in the off-white, beige, and taupe families are very popular and always in style—they are easily accessorized with a variety of colors. Anne is a firm subscriber to these neutrals; nearly all of her upholstered furniture is in varying shades of off-white. She can repaint the walls as frequently as she likes to create a whole new look without buying new furniture. She buys a few new accessories in her latest color passion, moves a few pieces of art around, and voilà, a brand new room.

But neutrals aren't just off-white, beige, and taupe anymore; much stronger colors can be neutral, too. Ochres, siennas, and umbers, deep colors from the yellow, orange, and brown families, are all warm, earthy colors and can provide a neutral backdrop. Just about any color can be considered a neutral when it is used in a deeper shade. Fire engine red might make your hair stand on end in a formal living room, but by adding black and turning it into a merlot, the red is toned down and made more soothing.

Opposite: Anne chose a rich chocolate for neutral walls in her master bedroom (Benjamin Moore Clinton Brown). Pumpkin and cognac colored textiles and accessories add warmth and comfort to the room.

Above: The soft patterns of the bed linens, from Restoration Hardware, pop off of the deep, rich, yet neutral Benjamin Moore Davenport Tan wall color.

*Benjamin Moore
Davenport Tan
HC-76*

*Benjamin Moore
Clinton Brown
HC-67*

Opposite and above: The Benjamin Moore Alexandria Beige walls in the kitchen make the perfect complement to the blues and browns of the great room. The aluminum Emeco Hudson Chairs by Philippe Starck (from Design Within Reach) are paired with a Donghia Supper Table and two upholstered settees.

*Benjamin Moore
Alexandria Beige
HC-77*

Tranquil colors elicit a soothing and calming environment and tend to be the softer, cooler tones of colors. Some of these color schemes include soft and muted greens, blues, grays, and beiges—think of sage green, hazy blue, steel gray, and sandy beige. Donna subscribes to this quiet, tranquil color palette and she uses a lot of monochromatic and low contrast colors to create soothing, feel-good environments.

Above: Behr Harvest Brown was used as a subtle backdrop for this sophisticated, yet understated living room. Varying shades and textures of taupe and beige fabrics were selected for the sofas and the occasional chairs which have been in the family for years

*Benjamin Moore
Palladian Blue
HC-144*

Below: The Benjamin Moore Palladian Blue walls of the great room set off the mocha and off-white accents. The sofas and chair are part of the Barbara Barry Collection for Baker.

Design Diary: New Neutrals

A friend once showed me a photograph from a magazine and said she wanted her room to look just like the picture. I told her it was easy to re-create this room because she already had most of the right furniture and accessories. All we'd need to do is to paint the walls a lovely shade of golden khaki. But, those words scared her to death, conjuring images of King Tut's tomb, and she refused. With time, and after showing her many photographs from books and magazines, I convinced her that this beautiful golden khaki was actually a new neutral and that it would make the mochas and persimmons in her floral and striped fabrics pop. Afterwards, I had to talk her out of painting every room in her house the same khaki!

Anne

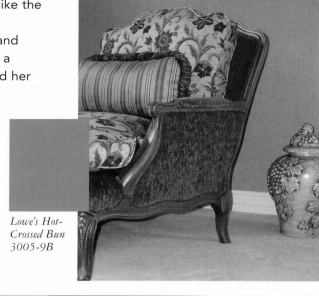

Lowe's Hot-Crossed Bun 3005-9B

BRIGHT COLORS

Bright colors feel strong and exciting. Some of the newest brights include chartreuse green, tangerine orange, fuchsia pink, and electric blue. Sometimes brights can be used together, as Anne did with her living room in Hong Kong—where fuchsia and tangerine fabrics and upholstery are set against color-washed lime green walls—a very striking and fresh look. Bright and intense colors can also be used sparingly as accents, which we both like to do in neutral or tranquil room settings.

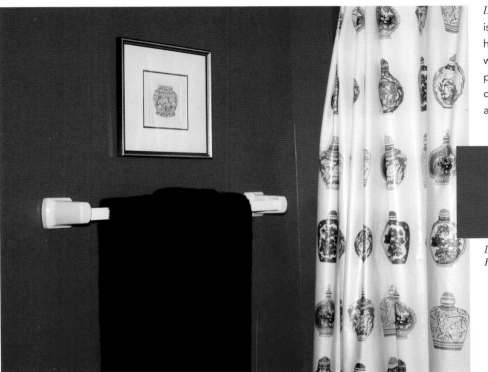

Left: Lowe's Brick Façade is the ideal wall color to highlight the blue and white Chinese snuff bottles pictured on the shower curtain, and the other bath accessories.

Lowe's Brick Façade 2002-3A

Lowe's Desert Grass 3008-7C

Right: Lowe's Desert Grass was the color chosen for this home office/guest room. The green silk cushions were purchased on sale and then enhanced with toile and trims. The shade for the floor lamp was re-covered with a black and white ticking fabric. The daybed was purchased from the Ballard Designs catalog. A collection of framed Vietnamese greeting cards hangs above the bed.

PAINTING 101

Overall a room only looks as good as the paint job itself. Hire the best painters you can afford! But if you're working within a budget or saving money for the new furniture, you can definitely do your own painting. Here are a few basic rules that we always follow in order to achieve the best results.

SELECTING PAINT, ROLLERS, AND BRUSHES

We like several paint brands, including: Benjamin Moore, ICI Dulux, Ralph Lauren, Lowe's American tradition, and Behr. One of our favorite painters, Sam Stone-Street, swears by Sherwin-Williams and refuses to use anything else. (He still hasn't forgiven us for those few occasions when we insisted he use another brand, because he couldn't get the color match just right.)

A hard and fast rule that we never break is using quality paintbrushes and rollers. They make a huge difference in the overall texture and quality of the paint job—and make the actual painting much easier. (They also last longer.) Make sure you select the appropriate paintbrush for the type of paint you will be using—don't use an oil paintbrush for latex paint and vice versa.

PREP WORK AND TIME PLANNING

Another rule we never break: you can never do enough prep work. The more time you spend preparing and getting organized, the less time you will spend painting. Don't think you're going to get the entire living room painted before you're off to a ballgame or the movies! Be prepared to budget a reasonable amount of time to accomplish the job.

Above and right: A simple coat of paint is all it took to enliven these rooms.

Do It: *Painting Basics*

nce you have all your supplies, do whatever prep work is required for the project, including: patching and sanding holes and imperfections (be sure to wipe off all the dust before painting), removing and/or covering furniture, removing electrical covers, and protecting the floor with drop cloths. Initially, you will want to use painter's tape around the windows, doors, and ceiling and floor moldings. If you're an expert painter with a lot of brush control, or you've learned how to handle an edger, the taping step can be skipped.

Difficulty Factor:
   Beginner/Intermediate
Time Factor: Hours
Materials and Supplies:
3" angled paintbrush
9" roller(s)
Cotton rags
Drop cloths
Edger
Hammer
Paint and primer
Paint trays
Painter's tape
Painter's wipes
Plastic cups
Putty knife
Sandpaper (medium, fine,
   very fine, extra fine)
Screwdriver
Spackle
Stirrers

Regardless of the wall color, it is almost always worth the effort to prime the walls first, as an underlying wall color can change the color of the new paint. Priming can also cut down on the number of coats required (sometimes you only need one), saving you time and money. If your wall color is at the lighter end of the spectrum, white primer is best. If your walls will be dark and deep, a lighter shade of the final color is often the best primer. Ask your paint seller which primer will work best for your paint.

Use a roller to cover most of the wall, and a brush for cutting in those areas a roller won't go—around windows, doors, floor and ceiling edges, and moldings. On our projects, Anne does the cutting in with a 3" Purdy angled brush, as it gives

her the control she needs to paint steady, clean edges. This requires a lot of practice and patience, so the less experienced will need to use painter's tape until the technique is perfected. Donna follows Anne with the roller, applying the paint everywhere else. Some people prefer to roll first and cut in after; the order is your preference.

TIP: Save Time Cleaning Paintbrushes
Wrap your brushes or rollers, with paint on them, in plastic wrap and place them in the freezer when you take a lunch break or go shopping for shoes, while the first coat of paint dries! When you're ready to start painting again, simply thaw the wrapped brushes by rubbing them with your warm hands for a few minutes, then unwrap them and start painting!

TIP: Save Time Cleaning Paint Trays
We like using disposable liners in our paint trays to make cleanup fast and easy.

The crown and baseboard moldings, painted an eye-catching fuchsia pink, tie together the window treatments and bedding in this guest room. The fuchsia pink and tangerine orange fabric of the window treatments is from Tricia Guild for Designers Guild.

BEYOND BASIC WALL PAINTING

When introducing color into a room, think beyond painting just the four walls and inject color in an unexpected way. What about painting just one wall? or the trim? or the ceiling? There are numerous options to explore; look through books and magazines for inspiration—we always do!

TRIM

Just about the fastest and easiest way to completely change the look of the room is to paint the trim. We paint trim in various ways, but most often, we use white or off-white semi-gloss paint, the most traditional approach and the safest. A second

option is to paint the trim a color that goes with the wall color: a beige wall with olive green trim, or taupe walls and chocolate brown trim. But the most dramatic effect is to leave the walls white or off-white and paint the trim a bold color, like true red, or hot pink, or black.

CEILINGS

Adding color to the ceiling can make a room feel larger or smaller, depending on the color used. High ceilings can be "brought down" by a darker color, making the room feel cozier and more intimate. Alternatively, a lower ceiling can seem higher and the room more open when painted a lighter

beautiful wallpaper in her powder room—a deep gold handwritten script pattern on an off-white background. But even with this beautiful wallpaper, the room seemed a bit lifeless. We achieved maximum impact when we painted the ceiling a deep metallic gold. The rich gold made all the difference in the world, breathing life into the room without dominating it.

ACCENT WALLS

One way to achieve color impact is to paint one or more walls a contrasting color. Our friend, Vinnie, has a large living room/dining room with a pair of columns that define the spaces. One dining room wall is painted cobalt blue and the opposite wall, in her living room, lime green. All the remaining walls are a bright off-white and serve as a dramatic backdrop for her amazing modern art collection. This technique of using two different bright colors on selected focal walls complements contemporary furnishings perfectly.

color. A ceiling painted with a lighter shade of the wall color visually extends the height of the walls.

A painted ceiling can do more than correct the visual disproportions of a room; it can be a lovely decorative technique as well. We had a client with

Above: The ceiling in this powder room was painted in a deep metallic gold to tie in with the wallpaper pattern and to heighten the visual impact of the room.

Right: The walls were painted neutral, while the crown and baseboard moldings were painted an unexpected color—black. The black and off-white color combination gives this media room a contemporary flavor.

STRIPES

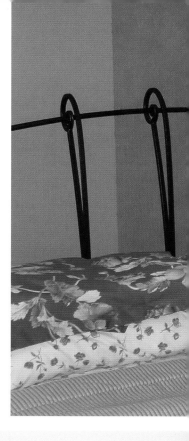

Stripes are a great way to make a statement in a room. They can be tonal (lighter and darker tones of the same color), contrasting (two different colors or two opposite colors), or a combination (several different colors).

The direction and size of the stripes make their own declaration. Vertical stripes tend to be more traditional and horizontal stripes lean towards the contemporary. Generally, the wider the stripe is, the more contemporary the effect.

Right: This cozy guest bedroom was given a basecoat of Lowe's Hot-Crossed Bun, then striped with a glaze of Ralph Lauren Teastain.

Lowe's Hot-Crossed Bun 3005-9B

Do It: *Painting Stripes*

Painting stripes on the wall isn't as difficult as it may seem. The easiest way is to first paint the entire room a base color, usually the lightest of the stripe colors.

Set a target size for the stripe width. For vertical stripes, measure the perimeter of the room and then divide the perimeter measurement by the stripe width. Tweak the stripe width until it divides evenly. For horizontal stripes, measure the height of the wall from floor molding to ceiling. Divide the height measurement by the stripe width. Tweak the stripe width until it divides evenly. If you're slightly off, for vertical stripes: add the extra amount to a stripe in a hidden corner; for horizontal stripes: add the extra amount to the bottom stripe.

Difficulty Factor: Intermediate
Time Factor: 2–3 Days
Materials and Supplies:
3" angled brush
9" rollers(s) for 10" stripes (Roller width should be narrower than stripe width.)
Chalk or #2 pencil
Drop cloths
Level
Measuring tape, ruler, or yardstick
Paints
Painter's tape
Painter's wipes
Screwdriver
Stirrers

For vertical stripes, it is imperative that the total number of stripes be an even number. Otherwise you'll end up with a double-sized last stripe. You can start vertical stripes anywhere in the room, because they can wrap around corners, flowing from one wall onto the next; they will not always end neatly in the corners.

For horizontal stripes, we prefer an odd number of stripes, which produces a top and bottom stripe in the same color. We often use the darker color for the first and last stripes to help ground them.

Using chalk and a 36" level, mark dots on the wall along the edges of each stripe every 12"–18". Then, connect the dots to draw solid lines the entire length of each stripe. Using painter's tape, place large X's in the

middle of every other stripe. The X'd stripes will not be painted.

Place lengths of painter's tape along the outside chalk-line edges of the stripes you want to paint, i.e., those without Xs. Roll or press the edges of the tape to prevent paint leakage. The hardest part is now complete.

Get out your paint or glaze and roller and start rolling between the taped edges. Pull off the masking tape before the paint or glaze dries. You can use painter's wipes for any small mistakes or mishaps. If you are applying additional color(s) or glaze to the unpainted stripes, repeat the above taping process.

TIP: Make the Edges Clean and Sharp
Be sure to seal the edges of the tape with a hard roller or your fingers to prevent the paint from leaking under the tape edge and creating a smudgy, uneven paint line.

Above: The bedding from Pottery Barn Kids was the inspiration for the three wide horizontal stripes painted all the way around this bedroom.

FAUX FINISHES

Faux finishes can be as simple as sponging, rolling, ragging, or pouncing a single color on the wall, or as elaborate as combining several of these techniques and using any number of colors. We prefer faux finishes that are more subtle, simple, muddled, and understated so the walls don't jump out and scream, "Look at me. I'm a faux painted wall!"

Benjamin Moore
Van Buren Brown
HC-70

Right: The walls were first painted with a nearly-chartreuse eggshell paint, then glazed with a mixture of deep red paint, glaze, and more than 50% water, which resulted in very warm, rich, and aged golden French Country walls.

Opposite: In this reading room, the walls were painted with Benjamin Moore Van Buren Brown and then glazed with Ralph Lauren Tobacco Aging Technique for added depth and richness. Bamboo floor matting was applied directly to the ceiling to complete the tranquil, Zen-like setting.

GLAZING

Glaze is an indispensable product for nearly any kind of faux finish and we use it for every finish we create. Paints mixed with glazes take longer to dry and have more "open time," giving you more time to work the technique.

Do It: *Mixing Glaze and Paint to Create a Faux Finish*

f you've never tried this technique before, we advise you first test it on some sample boards.

There are no hard and fast rules about mixing glazes. Take time to experiment with different glaze-to-paint ratios to see what works best for you. Our rule of thumb is: two parts glaze to one part paint. We also like to add water to our mixture as it dilutes it and makes it easier to work with. Make sure the glaze you buy is appropriate for the paint you are using (water vs. oil-based). Professional faux finishers generally use oil-based glazes, but we like water-based glazes because they're easier to clean up. Our favorite is Behr Faux Glaze.

Take time to practice your technique on sample boards, then, when you feel comfortable, test again on an inconspicuous area of the actual wall (behind the refrigerator, behind a large armoire or dresser, etc.). Allow time for the application to dry completely, as the effect looks totally different when wet.

Choose your base color carefully as it will be the predominant color of the faux finish. It is very

Difficulty Factor: Intermediate
Time Factor: 1–2 Days
Materials and Supplies:
1"–4" paintbrushes
4"–9" rollers
1"–4" throwaway paintbrushes (foam and bristle)
Drop cloths
Paints
Paint trays and liners
Painter's tape
Paint stirrers, many
Painter's wipes
Plastic cups
Plastic plates
Pouncing brush
Screwdriver
One or more of: sea sponge, rags, plastic wrap

important to use an eggshell paint, or, even better, a semi-gloss as the basecoat because the glossier the paint the longer the open time for applying glaze. It also makes it much easier to blend small sections as you work, leaving no obvious lines between work areas.

First, apply the main color haphazardly, using a standard-size roller, working in areas approximately 4' x 4'. Make sure the edges are uneven and irregular. Using small rollers, old paintbrushes, rags, plastic wrap, sea sponges, etc., immediately apply the pre-mixed accent color glaze(s) over the base. We often use three to four accent colors, mixed with varying amounts of glaze and/or water. The accent colors can be tones of the same color for a very subtle look, or complementary colors for a bit more drama. You may want to stick with one or two accent colors when you are starting out.

Now use the pouncing brush to blend the colors. To get the muddled and muted effect we like, a high-quality pouncing brush is critical. Keeping the bristles perpendicular to the wall, pounce the brush on the wall using small to medium taps, much like hammering a nail; don't use a standard stroking motion. And don't pounce everywhere; leave some areas untouched, as this adds to the muddled effect. Every so often, step back and take a look at your work from across the room to make sure you are achieving an overall consistency. This is especially important when more than one person is pouncing. You're finished when you think you are.

TIP: Leave Mistakes Alone While They're Still Wet!

If there is an area you're unhappy with, take our advice and leave it alone until it dries completely. The more you try to fix it while it is wet, the worse you will make it. It is much easier to come back after it has dried and use some watered-down paint and the pouncing brush to correct it.

The robins egg blue in
Georgie's dining room was
softened using an aging glaze
from Ralph Lauren.

Design Diary: Faux Finishing

Ralph Lauren Suede
Cheyenne Rock

A funny story—Anne had just moved to her new home in Texas and it was my first visit. Looking around her very large and very peach open kitchen and family room, I couldn't believe my eyes, but I knew the color must be there for a reason. Little did I know: the peach was just the basecoat; Anne had been waiting for my visit so I could help her with the faux finish. We selected the second base color, Ralph Lauren Suede Cheyenne Rock, knowing we wanted hints of the peach showing through to create another layer of depth. We used medium brown, pea green, and antique gold glazes, each mixed with Behr Faux Glaze and Ralph Lauren Teastain Glaze. This created six accent colors. But, by the time we finished, brushes and rollers had been used in various pots and cups, creating even more combinations! Six days and fifty hours later, our job was complete, and made the room feel warm and welcoming. So what are friends for anyway?

Donna

Left: A Ralph Lauren Suede paint, Cheyenne Rock, was used as the primary color in Anne's family room. Additional colors mixed with glaze included medium brown, pea green , and antique gold.

Above: The master bedroom was painted a deep red and washed with a very dark brownish black glaze, creating an incredibly rich tone suggestive of a ripe Bing cherry, just bitten into.

TIP: Paint Manufacturer's Directions Are Not the Final Word

When using specialty paints for any type of faux finish, you may need to ignore the manufacturer's application directions. This is especially true for paints with built-in finishes, such as Ralph Lauren Suede and River Rock Paints. Add these special-finish paints to your glaze mixtures the same way you would a regular paint.

TROMPE L'OEIL

Trompe l'oeil is a French term that means to "trick the eye" so that the viewer believes something that is painted is actually real! One of Anne's favorite trompe l'oeil effects is painted limestone blocks. The beauty of a painted limestone block wall is that it is flexible; it can be used in a formal or an informal setting and in most design styles, including contemporary, traditional, or eclectic. It can also be thought of as a neutral backdrop, and simultaneously as a focal wall. It can be left alone (our preference), or embellished with real or painted vines.

Below: Anne's dining room wall is the work of artist Amy Radford of Southlake, Texas. The faux weathered brick and stucco effect is the result of a collaboration of ideas and artistic talent.

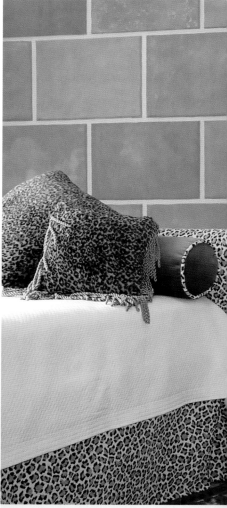

Above: This faux limestone block wall is in a guest bedroom/home office in Anne's home. Notice that the bottom blocks are larger in size, offering a visual anchor between the wall and floor.

Do It: *Painting the Limestone Block Wall*

Difficulty Factor:
Intermediate/Advanced

Time Factor: 2–5 Days, depending on area covered

Materials and Supplies:

4" or 5" disposable rollers

1"–4" paintbrushes

9" rollers (1 per color)

1"–4" throwaway brushes (foam and bristle)

Artist brush (thin)

Chalk or #2 pencil

Drop cloths

Feather

Glaze

Level

Paints (3 or more colors)

Paint stirrers, many

Painter's tape

Paint trays

Painter's wipes

Pastel crayons

Plastic plates

Pouncing brush

Sample board

Screwdriver

Tape measure, ruler, or yardstick

One or more of: sea sponge, rags, plastic wrap

the grout lines. Measure the height of the wall, from floor molding to ceiling, and divide it by the height of the block plus one grout line. Tweak the block size until it divides evenly. If you're slightly off, just add the difference to the bottom row of blocks. Next, measure the width of the wall from corner to corner. Divide it by the block width plus one grout line, tweaking the block width until it divides evenly.

Using these measurements as a guide, paint the horizontal and vertical grout lines onto the wall using a 4" or 5" disposable roller. You can mark chalk guides on the wall and eyeball the straight lines of the grout, as you will be rolling with a much wider roller than the actual grout width. You may end up lucky, as we have on occasion, and the existing wall color will be perfect for the grout color. *Very Important:* Make sure that you use flat paint for the grout lines you paint, as it's easily covered by the other paints and faux finishes you'll use when you paint the limestone blocks themselves.

Once all the grout lines are painted, you are ready to start painting the blocks. This process is actually much easier to do than it is to explain, so please don't be daunted by the detailed instructions that follow.

lthough extremely time consuming, limestone block walls are a fairly easy project to tackle once you have mastered mixing and applying glazes. You'll want to practice a bit on some sample boards. When you get to the actual walls, it'll be easier (and a lot more fun) with the help of a friend or two.

First, determine the size of your blocks (scale is important here). We like a block that is 11"–14" wide x 8"–11" high. Next, determine the width of

. . . .

TIP: Shop for Paint in the "OOPS" Bin
Many local home improvement centers and paint stores have an "oops" bin, which has a wide variety of custom-mixed colors made by mistake. These are perfect paints for a faux painting project, and they are available at deeply discounted prices!

The Limestone Block Wall (continued)

1. Begin with the bottom row of blocks. Place painter's tape horizontally along outside bottom edges of blocks, all the way across the wall (on the bottom row, the tape will cover the baseboard molding).

2. Place painter's tape horizontally along outside top edges of the bottom row of blocks (this will protect the grout between rows 1 and 2 as well as part of the blocks in row 2).

3. Place painter's tape vertically along the two remaining outside edges (left and right sides) of the first block in bottom row. Continue placing painter's tape vertically along right and left outside edges of every other block in the first row (3rd, 5th, 7th, etc., blocks.)

4. Once every other block in bottom row is taped on all four sides, you can paint each taped block with the base color, using a brush or roller. Immediately follow with the limestone faux painting technique (see page 53), while the basecoat is still wet.

5. After every other block on bottom row is painted with base color and faux finish, repeat the same taping and painting process on every other row going up the wall (rows 3, 5, 7, etc.) until every other block, in every other row, is painted to resemble a limestone block.

6. Go back to the bottom row and remove vertical tape pieces only.

7. Apply painter's tape vertically on outside edges of blocks that have not yet been painted (the 2nd, 4th, 6th, 8th, etc. blocks in rows 1, 3, 5, 7, etc.).

8. Once this round of taping is complete, apply base paint color and faux finish to these blocks. Now, all the blocks in rows 1, 3, 5, 7, etc., are painted.

9. Remove all horizontal tape pieces from rows, beginning at bottom row. Apply new horizontal pieces of tape along outside edges of blocks in rows 2, 4, 5, 8, etc. This new horizontal taping will cover grout lines and some of the painted blocks in rows 1, 3, 5, 7, etc.

10. Apply vertical tape pieces to the right and left outside edges of every other block (1st, 3rd, 5th, 7th, etc., blocks in rows 2, 4, 5, 8, etc.), just as you did when you taped every other block in the odd numbered rows. Once every other block is taped on all four outside edges, you can apply base paint and faux finish to these blocks.

11. After painting every other block in rows 2, 4, 6, 8, etc., go back to the bottom (2nd) row and remove vertical tape pieces only.

12. Apply painter's tape vertically on outside edges of blocks that have not yet been painted (2nd, 4th, 6th, 8th, etc., blocks in rows 2, 4, 6, 8, etc.). Apply base paint color and faux finish to these blocks. Now all blocks in rows 2, 4, 6, 8, etc., in fact, all blocks on the wall, are painted and faux-finished. The hardest part is over and there are only a few final steps to complete the limestone blocks.

To make the faux finish mixtures you'll apply over the basecoat, follow the instructions discussed on page 48. We like to use browns, beiges, taupes, and creams in our limestone faux finishes.

There is no one correct way to apply the faux finish to the blocks. We use an array of brushes and sponges, and apply the glaze mixtures in a variety of ways: we roll them on, streak them on, dry-brush them on, pounce them on, plastic wrap them on, you name it! Begin with the base color mixture then add and blend secondary and other highlight colors over one another. (We like to start with the lightest highlight tones and work up to the darker shades.) You can use a thin artist's brush, or a feather, to lightly trace some cracks in the stone. Add very subtle pockmarks with the tip of a sea sponge.

You can leave the painter's tape on the wall for up to two weeks, so you can take your time and come back to the project whenever you like. (Remember our frozen paintbrush tip.)

After the entire wall is finished and you've removed the tape, you can add shadow lines to the blocks, which makes them look even more realistic. Draw very thin lines with medium brown pastel crayon and smudge them with an old rag. The shadow lines will fall on one horizontal and one adjoining vertical edge of each block, depending on the direction of the natural light in the room. If there are high windows to the left of the blocks, the shadow lines will be on the right and bottom edges of the blocks. If the windows are lower and to the right of the blocks, the shadows will fall on the left and top edges of the blocks. Lastly, depending on the look you're after, you can apply a coat of glaze (we like Ralph Lauren Sunfade or Teastain) to add even more depth. This will also help to protect the smudge lines.

Opposite: The faux limestone block wall in this television room was intentionally left unadorned, because the wall treatment is the "art." Most of the paint colors were found in the "oops" bin of the local home improvement center (see page 53 for more on the "oops" bin).

Above: Faux limestone blocks painted on a kitchen island help to disguise scuffmarks and nicks resulting from everyday use.

MURALS

Murals are beautiful pieces of art painted directly on a wall, ceiling, art niche, or even a closet door. Many people think murals belong only in a child's room, a baby's nursery, or a dining room. Although murals are wonderful in those settings, they can be just as scene-stealing in other rooms in the home. They can be painted onto the main wall, or wrap all the way around the room. Sometimes just a small area painted with something special is the perfect accent or surprise for a room.

Below: A mural of a traditional English hunting scene, in a medley of soft blues and greens, dresses up what would otherwise be a simple white dining room.

Right: Even a very simple design can add a unique touch to a room. Here, assorted paints and glazes were used to embellish the arched exit to this master bedroom.

Do It: *Tips for Painting Murals*

Difficulty Factor:
Beginner/Intermediate/
Advanced

Time Factor: Minutes to
Days, depending on
size of area

Materials and Supplies:

Only some of these sup-
plies may be required.
Read on for further
instructions.

4"–9" rollers

1"–4" throwaway brushes
(foam and bristle)

Acrylic paints (2 oz. plastic containers of various
colors)

Artist brushes (inexpen-
sive ones in various
sizes; even children's
brushes are okay)

Carbon paper and pencil

Chalk

Drop cloths

Glazes or sealants

Plastic plates

Pastel crayons

Overhead projector

Pouncing brush

Plastic plates

Paints

Paint stirrers (many)

Paint trays and liners

Painter's chalk

Painter's markers

Painter's tape

Painter's wipes

Screwdriver

Spray fixative

Tape measure, ruler, or
yardstick

Watercolor pencils

One or more of: sea
sponge, feather, rags,
plastic wrap

lthough an artist's mural is second to none, crafty or creative people can also take on the challenge of painting a mural. If you don't feel confident enough to freehand your drawing, here are some of the shortcuts that have worked for us:

- Use an overhead projector to project any two-dimensional image directly onto the wall, then trace all lines with chalk or pencil.
- Trace artwork onto the wall using carbon paper: Place carbon-side to wall; tape; tape artwork (photograph, drawing, design) over carbon paper. Using a fair amount of pressure on your pencil, trace over lines of art, transferring them to the wall.
- Use purchased stencils and stenciling kits.

You can use any kind of paint in your mural, including acrylics. If you have traced artwork, use the original as your guide for colors and shadows. Remember, if you make a mistake, you can paint over it and try again. When you have the result you want, you may want to spray your finished mural with a spray fixative, or cover it with a clear sealant.

Missy stenciled her master bathroom walls and then added a glaze for an aged effect. For a finishing touch, she painted the ceiling a deep, rich gold.

Above: A Moroccan tent was the inspiration for the mural in this small transitional hallway.

Below: We recently tackled the Ralph Lauren Denim Finish for the very first time. We purchased the kit and followed the instructions—it was easy and fairly straightforward, although somewhat time consuming. The finished look is fun and can go in just about any room.

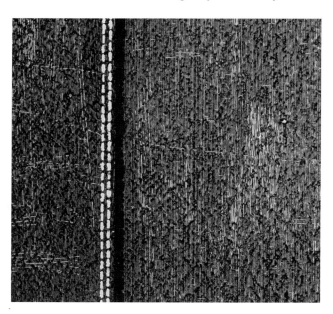

3D IDEAS

To create a unique mural, think in 3D. In the bedroom of a little girl who dreamed of a castle on a hillside, we painted the perimeter of the room to look like a valley full of blooming flowers. For the 3D effect, we whitewashed an actual picket fence and installed it over the mural. Then we added a rope swing hanging from the branches of a tree painted in a corner. We've also strung a rope hammock between two palm trees painted on adjacent walls, the perfect spot for a cache of stuffed animals.

Above: A close-up of a lifelike mural in Bella's bedroom painted by artists Barbara McBurney and Diane Gates of Texas. The artists intentionally incorporated the window-seat into the mural.

Right: A hand-painted mural of an outdoor canopy covers the entire ceiling and the top of the four walls of this little girl's bedroom. You can practically feel the breeze gently blowing the canopy cover.

Opposite: Bruno and John's playroom has a wild jungle theme—just perfect for two little brothers. It is the work of artist Rachel Palmer.

CHAPTER 2

THE PAPERED WALL

Wallpaper, like most things, comes and goes in and out of style. Today, wallpaper has made a comeback. Perhaps this is because there are so many different kinds of wallpaper available, including: vinyl, grass, metallic and metal leaf, leather look, and various handmade papers. Never before have so many choices been available.

Oppositet and above: Classic and elegant, this Schumacher wallpaper sets off the rich elegance of this traditional dining room.

PREPARING TO WALLPAPER

When talking about wallpaper, we can't omit the necessary evil that goes along with it: prep work. There is always some kind of tedious prep work to do before you can begin wallpapering, including removing old wallpaper, preparing the surface, and sizing the wall.

Opposite: The green and red toile Pierre Deux wallpaper is the perfect choice for the eating area of this French Country kitchen.

Below: A more formal toile wallpaper dresses up this powder room.

If you plan to hang wallpaper on a wall that has never been wallpapered before, you're in luck—you get to skip this step. Removing old wallpaper is time consuming and labor intensive, so consider hiring a professional for the job. If you decide to remove the wallpaper yourself, please follow the advice of our wallpaper guru David Stevens of Stevens Paint and Wallpaper in Baton Rouge, Louisiana. David is a third generation tradesman with a lifetime of experience working alongside his father and grandfather in the family's 80-year-old business. Here are three of his favorite techniques for those who want to tackle the job on their own.

Opposite top: This bright pink and green Pierre Deux toile wallpaper is the backdrop for the powder room servicing the kitchen and informal areas of the home.

Opposite bottom: The Asian inspired toile wallpaper really dresses up this bath.

Do It: *Wallpaper Removal Techniques*

Dry Removal Method

Some papers can actually be removed more easily when they are dry. Lift an edge of the wallpaper and pull it away from the wall; try pulling in different directions. If the paper comes off in large pieces, the dry removal method should work for you. If you find it pulls away more easily in any particular direction, pull all the paper off in that direction. If you don't get nice, large pieces when you pull, you'll have to try a different method.

Tap Water Removal Method

Often, the best tool for removing wallpaper is plain tap water. Using a spray bottle or a soaked sponge, test an area to see if the paper will absorb the water. Be sure to apply plenty of water over a five to ten minute span. Using a wallpaper scorer before wetting can help the paper absorb the water; just don't press too hard and score the wall itself. If the paper pulls away from the wall in large pieces after

Difficulty Factor: Easy to Difficult
Time: 1–3 Days
Materials and Supplies:
Only some of these supplies may be required. Read on for further instructions.
Industrial steamer
Sponges
Scrapers (6")
Spray bottle
Wallpaper scorer
Water
Water-soluble wallpaper removal solution
White vinegar

soaking, then go ahead and wet down all the wallpaper. Remove it using a 6-inch scraper and a sponge, being very careful not to gouge the wall. You may need to continually wet the wallpaper to keep it moist enough for removal.

Wallpaper Removal Products

If you find that the dry and tap water methods don't work for you, consider using a wallpaper removal product. There are a few different types available. The first is a water-soluble solution that seeps in and relaxes old wallpaper and paste residue, making it easier to remove with a scraper. Popular brands include DIF and 3M. Alternatively, many people have reported success using plain white vinegar.

You can also rent a commercial steamer. (Be sure to score the paper first.) Some people report success using steamers, but neither of us has had much luck with them and they can be costly, too.

When John and I purchased our very first home, which was nearly 80 years old, we agreed that the first two things that needed to go were the kitchen's extremely ugly and outdated wallpaper and its worn and peeling linoleum floor. I tackled the wallpaper and John the floor. I soon discovered not just one, but three layers of wallpaper! I painstakingly stripped it in very small sections, and grew more and more impatient as the day(s) progressed. John was having nearly the same results with the floor. We both plowed ahead ever so slowly when, on the third weekend, John hit the mother load—the original hardwood kitchen floor! So, envious of John's success, I got quite aggressive with my removal technique. Soon, I was tearing off small slivers of the wall. Then, the slivers turned into chunks and the chunks into slabs! John stopped me dead in my tracks; it was time to hire a professional—Mr. Bob Mayfield. Bob took one look at the nightmare I'd created and told us it would now cost more to fix my mistakes than it would have if we'd just hired him from the start. He also asked if he could use me as a reference for "how not to strip wallpaper"!

Anne

TIP: If You're Looking for New Wallpaper, Consider a Peelable Vinyl

Peelable vinyl wallpaper (which is very popular) is one of the easiest to remove. The first layer just peels off the wall, no water or mixes required, leaving a backing paper adhered to the wall. Soak the backing paper with water and remove it with a sponge or scraper.

PREPPING THE WALL

Once all the wallpaper is removed, it's time to create a smooth wall surface. Smooth walls offer better wallpaper adhesion, tighter seams, and a nicer overall finished look. If you haven't done too much damage removing the old wallpaper, you'll be able to tackle the wall prep yourself. Take time to do the job properly, as wall areas not adequately smoothed will stand out like a sore thumb once the wallpaper is hung.

For slight imperfections here and there, a little spackle, a putty knife, and sandpaper will do the trick. Working in small areas, fill in any holes and dings with spackle, then smooth them with a scraper slightly wider than the area you are cover-

ing. You may need to repeat this step a few times. After the spackle dries, sand it with medium-grade sandpaper, followed by a fine-grade. Be sure to carefully wipe off all sanding dust with a damp cloth or a tacking cloth.

For more than just minor touch-ups, or for walls with textured finishes, such as knock down and orange peel, a little spackle just won't do the job. Smoothing these walls requires "skim coating" with joint compound or plaster, which fills the pocks and valleys to create a smooth, even surface. This may sound easy—and for a seasoned pro, it is. So our advice is to hire a drywall professional. It is affordable, and well worth the investment.

SIZING

There is one last prep task that will make the wallpaper go up much more easily—applying wallpaper sizing to the walls. Sizing looks like paint, comes in a paint can, and is applied with a roller or brush just like paint. It gives walls a light gloss making the wallpaper easier to move around. Sizing also helps wallpaper removal down the road. You may not need sizing if your walls are primed with a fresh non-latex primer. (David Stevens cautions that fresh latex paint will blister and peel under wallpaper, causing it to bubble.) Sizing is relatively inexpensive and is easy to apply. If you are not sure whether your walls need it, be safe rather than sorry, and apply it.

SELECTING WALLPAPER

Generally speaking, spend as much money on wallpaper as you can afford. Cheap wallpaper tends to looks cheap—even more so once it's hung. But this doesn't mean that the most expensive wallpaper is always the best. There are many wallpaper options out there for all budgets and tastes, each with its own pros and cons.

Opposite: The script handwriting of the wallpaper softens this all black and off-white master bath.

Above: The guest bath was covered with a solid grayish-taupe wallpaper that resembles an elephant's skin.

VINYL-COATED WALLPAPER

The most common kind of wallpaper available today is vinyl-coated wallpaper—paper coated with vinyl or acrylic. It is durable and, because it can be lightly scrubbed with mild soap and water, it is ideal for kitchens and bathrooms. (Before scrubbing the wallpaper the first time, test it in an inconspicuous area.) Although vinyl-coated wallpaper tends to have a shiny finish, this hasn't kept us from using it many, many times.

FABRIC-COATED WALLPAPER

Fabric-coated wallpaper—fabric coated with a vinyl or acrylic coating—is also quite popular. The pattern is printed directly on the coating, not the fabric underneath. This wallpaper is somewhat porous, and shouldn't be used in kitchens and baths, though some varieties are considered "washable" and can be cleaned with a soft sponge and mild soap and water. (Don't confuse washable with scrubbable!) There are many gorgeous fabric-coated wallpapers out there, but they tend to be a bit more expensive.

PAPER-BACKED FABRIC WALLPAPER

Paper-backed fabric wallpaper (another common variety) is exactly what the name implies—fabric backed with paper. This wallpaper gives the walls an upholstered look, but with the relative ease of hanging wallpaper, rather than the more involved process of covering walls with fabric (which we discuss in Chapter 3).

NATURAL FIBER WALLPAPER

Natural fiber wallpaper is one of our favorites. It is made from a natural fiber with a paper backing, making it easier to install than the natural fiber alone would be. Some of these natural fibers include: jute, sisal, hemp, seagrass, burlap, coir, cotton, linen, and wool. Because these papers require a bit more maintenance, they should be used in low traffic areas. They are also more difficult to patch if an accident occurs and tend to be somewhat pricey.

Opposite: This green and red toile Pierre Deux wallpaper is as at home in a kitchen as in a living room.

Left: Donghia natural wallpaper enhances the quiet sophistication of a contemporary bathroom. The woven texture is a lovely compliment to the smooth porcelain and tile surfaces and the calming accessories.

HAND-PRINTED WALLPAPER

Just as the name implies, this type of wallpaper is printed by hand. It comes in untrimmed rolls; it has a one- or two-inch selvage on the side edges, which must be trimmed off, either on the wall or on a paperhanger's table. The selvage protects the edges from being damaged during shipping. Untrimmed paper requires more skill to hang and costs more to have installed. These papers tend to be the most expensive, and they are not washable or scrubbable. But, don't let these details scare you away. Consider using it sparingly—on only a focal wall or just on the inside of paneled molding. Or create a paneled molding appearance by framing the wallpaper with fluted or architectural moldings.

PRE-TRIMMED AND PRE-PASTED WALLPAPER

With the exception of hand-printed wallpaper, all the wallpapers described are pre-trimmed, meaning the sides are cut at the factory and should match when hung. Occasionally, these papers are incorrectly trimmed at the factory and the seams will not match. In this case, you'll either have to hand-trim the edges yourself, or better, return the wallpaper. Most wallpaper (except the hand-painted variety) is pre-pasted, meaning there is already wallpaper paste on the backing; you just need to add water to activate it. Most professionals use some type of wallpaper paste anyway. It is best to speak with your wallpaper supplier about your specific needs.

NATURAL MATERIALS

We are very drawn to the less traditional wallpapers—those made of natural materials, such as paper, fiber, reed, cork, and grass. There are many benefits to using natural wall coverings: they absorb noise, help hide wall imperfections, add texture, are environmentally friendly, and bring the outdoors in! While some consider these papers to be a bit more contemporary, they can in fact look quite nice in a more traditional or even formal setting, and they can take the edge off a stuffy room.

Above left: Thibaut's jungle leaf themed wallpaper adds a dramatic flourish to a small powder bath.

Above right: Magnolia leaf wallpaper invigorates this master bath suite.

Opposite: The grasscloth wallpaper coordinates effortlessly with the other natural products in this kitchen, including the burlap window treatments and the tumbled marble.

PATTERNS FOUND IN NATURE

f the product itself is not made of a natural material, we favor those that are inspired by nature: flora, fauna, and rocks, minerals and metals.

PLANTS AND FLOWERS

Among the more traditional wallpapers, we lean toward leaves, flowers, vines, silk strie, and Asian toile. They are beautiful and simple and even larger prints, such as the huge leaves from a banana tree, can be fresh and simple. We like to use these papers in smaller rooms, such as a powder room or a butler's pantry.

ANIMALS

We also love wallpapers inspired by animals—like leathers (cow hides, snake skins, crocodile, or alligator skins), leopard or zebra prints, or any other animal hide or skin. Although animal prints have been "in" lately, take note: they are truly a classic style and never go out of fashion. They are perfectly at home in any environment, even a very traditional home.

Right: The palm trees and monkeys of this Schumacher wallpaper print are reminiscent of a family vacation to Malaysia.

Below: Anne uses pumpkin and chocolate accessories to complement the Schumacher leopard print wallpaper in the master bath.

A close-up of wallpaper resembling stone. The wallpaper gets its contemporary look from the fact that the stone is laid square instead of the more traditional staggered approach.

ROCKS AND METALS

Other wallpaper inspirations found in nature are rocks and metals. Think of limestone, marble, granite, or sand, as well as gold, silver, or copper. These wallpapers should be used sparingly and the wallpaper itself should be of fairly good quality; otherwise, it tends to look cheap and unrealistic. Think of a focal wall covered in limestone block wallpaper, or a powder bath covered in wallpaper of silver leaf squares.

PARTIAL WALLPAPERING

Instead of wallpapering an entire room, consider papering just one wall or a ceiling, or using multiple wallpapers in a room! We love ceilings papered in a natural wallpaper (cork, grasscloth, or even burlap), which creates a unique look without detracting from the walls or artwork. It is also a great trick for covering up flaws—cracks, water damage, or an uneven ceiling. Create a focal wall by installing wallpaper on just one wall in a room. In a master bedroom, an obvious choice is the wall behind the bed. In a dining room, the wall behind the server is a good option.

Above: The wallpaper applied to the wall behind the bed sets the sensual and exotic tone in this master bedroom.

Opposite: Carleton V limestone block wallpaper highlights the focal wall of a contemporary yet classic master bedroom. The furniture is from Bernhardt's Paris Collection.

As for wallpaper borders, although we don't really care for them, there are some lovely wallpaper borders out there. We have had numerous clients insist on using them, and we are always happy to oblige, trying to use them in unique or unexpected ways.

Placement of the border is key. Try it one third of the way down from the ceiling, or halfway between the ceiling and floor to make the look more special. A few years ago, we applied a border of ballet slippers and tutus midway over light pink color-washed walls. To this day, it remains one of our favorites. Far more unexpected, we once placed a border around a powder room window, enhancing the simple white plantation shutters. And we've created a tray ceiling effect by placing multiple borders around the perimeter of a dining room ceiling (note: not the upper wall).

ALTERNATIVE MATERIALS

Other kinds of paper can be applied directly to walls or ceilings with wallpaper paste. Consider especially papers relating to the use of a room. In a study, we installed retro maps of assorted colors directly onto the ceiling, in an overlapping fashion. Black-and-white maps would be a great choice for a traditional study or a contemporary home office. Film posters make great wallpaper in a media room. Donna suggests using old devalued stock certificates or *Wall Street Journal* pages in a home office. If wine is your passion, consider wine labels; and for travel afficianados, now you have something to do with all those travel papers and souvenirs. All of these papers can be sealed with natural or color-based polyurethane to enhance or age the look, or, left as is.

Opposite: Kraft paper was applied directly over outdated wallpaper and only below the chair rail in this dining room. The wall was sealed with a coat of an oil-based polyurethane clear stain.

Left: The retro maps were purchased on eBay and applied to the ceiling in an overlapping style. The Philippe Starck Louis Ghost Chair is nearly invisible against the wood tones of the cabinetry and floor. Chocolate brown cork is used as a bulletin board behind the computer monitor.

KRAFT PAPER

Kraft paper, postal wrap, or brown paper grocery bags take on a new life when treated as wallpaper. Brown bagging, as we like to call it, has a fabulous look and is an inexpensive and easy technique to learn. It's a natural product, which adds to its freshness and uniqueness. Not only is it at home in any decorating style, it is also at home in any room—"dressed-up" in a formal dining room or "dressed-down" in a bathroom or laundry room. Depending on the paper and who's doing the application, the look achieved can vary from informal (in its natural state) to that of a high-end designer leather or stone (after a layer or two of polyurethane). You can also brown bag with tissue paper, newspaper (Asian newspaper is one of our favorites), magazines, or wrapping paper.

Do It: *Brown Bagging a Wall*

his project is actually very easy to do, especially with a friend or two; you will get the hang of it in 15–30 minutes. Start with two rolls of paper. Once you have applied them, you'll know the total number of rolls you'll need to finish the job.

Label two garbage bags, naming one "straight edges", and the other "torn edges". Tear paper into irregular shapes of various sizes, crumple them into loose balls, and put the balls in the appropriate garbage bag (straight edges are pieces torn from the clean-edged sides of the roll; torn edges are all other pieces). The straight-edge pieces will be used along ceilings, baseboards, and around doors and windows. You can apply the straight and torn pieces in any order.

This is where a friend or two comes in handy. Remove a piece of paper, loosely smooth it open

Difficulty Factor: Beginner/Intermediate/Advanced
Time Factor: 1–2 Days
Materials and Supplies:
4"–5" paintbrush (straight-edged)
Cotton rags
Garbage bags (large)
Kraft paper or brown postal wrap
Ladder
Polyurethane (oil- or water-based; optional)
Table top
Wallpaper paste
Wallpaper brush
A friend or more (optional)

with your hand, apply wallpaper paste to either side, and then place it on the wall. Neatness does not count—you can apply the paper to the wall with as few or as many creases as you want.

Left: An old dining room server and mirror were converted into a bathroom vanity. The walls were treated with the brown bag technique, and then given a topcoat of polyurethane. Note the strip of fabric découpaged and polyurethanted behind the sink to serve as a backsplash.

Opposite, left and right: Torn Kraft paper was applied above and below the chair rail in this otherwise traditional dining room. The Kraft paper was left natural and intentionally not sealed.

Neatness is very important, however, when installing the straight edges around doors, windows, and moldings, as you want to make one long straight continuous line. Overlap them as little or as much as you like. It doesn't matter which side of the paper is applied, nor does it matter if extra paste leaks out and onto the paper or wall—all of this will enhance the end result.

Allow the work to dry at least overnight before applying a finish coat of oil-based polyurethane with a paintbrush. Minwax clear is one we like, but tinted polyurethanes work well, too. (You can also use water-based polyurethane, but we like the finish and depth of an oil-based finish. It's also more water repellant.) Don't panic when you apply the polyurethane, as the walls will immediately become darker; they will lighten and soften after they dry. You can skip the polyurethane if you want a softer, subtler effect.

TIP: Gigi's Brown Paper Bag Technique
Our friend Gigi created her own look by gathering brown paper from several sources: postal wraps, butcher's paper, painter's paper, and even grocery bags. Her result is much more dramatic, adding even more contrast and depth to the layers.

TIP: Brown Paper Bag Variations
A few variations that can be added to the brown bag technique include: torn shopping bag labels, travel memorabilia, or wine labels.

Kraft paper was applied directly over the outdated wallpaper above the chair rail and sealed with a top-coat of oil-based polyeurethane. The seagrass floor rug enhances the natural character of the setting.

Design Diary: Brown Bagging

One of our fondest brown bagging memories was with four of our favorite clients: Steve, Terri, and their sons, Barrett and Breuer. The family was building their dream home and were thrilled with the idea of brown bagging the powder room. One Friday night, as Anne and I were in the midst of working, the family arrived with gourmet pizza and we all had a picnic on the dining room floor. Afterwards Anne and I reluctantly got back to work. When Barrett and Breuer heard us laughing as we worked, we suddenly had two new assistants. Barrett, the 12 year old, applied the wallpaper paste, and Breuer, the 6 year old, applied the paper to the walls. Little did they know, they helped us complete the job in half the time! And it made the boys a part of building their new home.

Donna

Design Diary: Brown Bagging

I convinced my husband that we needed to brown bag my small office off the kitchen, and asked him for his help. Soon after we started, John pointed out that he was the grunt worker, applying the paste, and I was the artist, applying the bags to the wall. Regardless, we had a great time and the entire project took only about three hours. John was most amazed that the whole thing only cost $23.00. Unbeknownst to him, I had the old, solid door replaced with custom-made French doors to the tune of $800.00!

Anne

CHAPTER 3

THE OTHER WALL

While most painted and papered walls are flat in appearance, what we call the "other" wall uses texture and dimension as its key elements. Most newly built homes feature standard wall textures, such as orange peel or knock down, which builders use to make wall and ceiling finishes consistent and to disguise wall imperfections. In contrast to these standards, there are various other wall textures you can create yourself, from old techniques that have found new life (hand-troweled and Venetian plaster walls) to original and imaginative ways to use fabric on walls, to new twists on looks that could otherwise seem dated: brick, paneling, stone, tile, and rock.

Opposite and above: The walls in the formal areas were hand troweled with plaster, painted using a taupe eggshell oil-based paint, and then finished with a brown oil-based glaze for added luster. The same finish was applied not only to the walls, but also to the ceiling.

THE HAND-TROWELED WALL

One of the most popular walls these days is the hand-troweled wall. Although people have been hand troweling walls for centuries, it used to be a much more difficult project than it is with today's new troweling materials. You can achieve the hand-troweled look with several different materials: joint compound, plaster, and Venetian plaster. Each method has its own advantages and disadvantages. Although still somewhat time consuming, the application techniques are not that hard to do; basically, if you can ice a cake, you can hand-trowel a wall! Joint compound is the easiest material to use, and the one we recommend for beginners.

Opposite: Hand-troweled plaster walls complement the wood tones of the island and cabinets.

Design Diary:
Hand Troweling

My husband and I have moved and redecorated several homes over the last few years. Each time my Mom comes to visit our newest home she asks whether I bought new living room furniture. This last time she asked, I replied, "No Mom, It's the same old furniture, it just feels new because I hand-troweled the walls with plaster, then painted and glazed, and added a new rug and pillows." She is always amazed with how different my furniture looks by simply changing the walls.

Anne

HAND-TROWELING
WITH JOINT COMPOUND

Before you hand-trowel joint compound or plaster on the wall, it is a good idea to test your application techniques, colors, and glazes on sample boards. You can use foam board, cardboard, leftover drywall, or sheetrock, or any other building supplies you may have around.

The walls were hand-troweled using joint compound, then painted, and finally, glazed with a Ralph Lauren Aging Technique.

Do It: *Making Hand-troweled Joint Compound Sample Boards*

Perhaps the least expensive material to hand-trowel is joint compound. You can use any type of joint compound; it comes in both pre-mixed and powder forms. Although the pre-mixed is a bit more expensive, we prefer it because it is less messy and less time consuming. Joint compound can be purchased in any home improvement center or local hardware store.

The authenticity of the final appearance is a direct result of how the material is applied, and you'll want to try out various combinations. In general, if you want your walls to look chunky and a bit more casual or rustic, apply a larger amount of the compound in a haphazard fashion, holding your trowel at a higher angle, making a lot of peaks. For a softer and subtler look, apply a little less compound and hold the trowel at a lower angle, creating fewer peaks.

Paint your sample board the same color as your walls.

Scoop some joint compound onto a trowel— we use trowels ranging from 4"-12", depending on the look we're after. (Wider trowels create a smoother surface with fewer trowel lines; narrower trowels produce more trowel lines and a chunkier appearance.) Slap the joint compound directly onto the sample board, then begin moving it around, squishing, pushing, twisting, and pulling, experimenting with different compound thicknesses, trowel sizes, trowel angles, and trowel motions.

When the compound is dry, paint over it with the paint color you've selected using an extra thick nap roller to cover the peaks and valleys of the compound. When the paint has dried, you may want to add a topcoat of glaze, such as one of the Ralph Lauren Aging Technique Glazes. (We tend to favor Teastain, as it looks good with most colors.) Or, tint or shade a clear glaze with a deeper shade of your paint color. Use a thick nap roller to apply the glaze. Remember, if you plan to apply any kind of glaze topcoat, it is important to use a semi-gloss paint for the basecoat.

After the paint and glaze layers dry, you will have several sample board options. Take time to look at them from different places and distances, as the look will vary depending on light and perspective.

Difficulty Factor:
  Beginner/Intermediate/
  Advanced
Time Factor: half-hour to an
  hour
Materials and Supplies:
4"- 12" trowels (2 or 3)
Glaze (optional)
Paint
Roller (extra thick nap)
Sample boards

TIP: Cut Corners for the Experienced
If you are more experienced with a hand trowel, you could make a large test area directly on the wall, in an inconspicuous place like behind the refrigerator or in the garage. The disadvantage to testing this way is that you won't have samples to move around.

Do It: *Creating the Painted and Glazed Joint Compound Wall*

You will use the same techniques to apply joint compound to your walls that you used on the sample boards. If you are applying the compound over old wallpaper, first lightly score the walls with a wallpaper scorer. Then apply painter's tape where necessary: around doors, windows, ceilings, and baseboard moldings. The compound can be applied directly to most other walls without preparation.

After mixing the compound, begin your hand-troweling on the most inconspicuous wall in the room. Scoop some compound out with your trowel or transfer it to the trowel with a putty knife. Apply a glob of compound about the size of your fist directly to the wall. Spread it around in a sweeping, back and forth motion keeping the layer anywhere from $1/16$- to $1/3$-inch thick, squishing, pushing, twisting, and pulling the compound as you did on the practice boards. Keep adding more globs and continue to spread.

Next, begin lightly tapping the compound with the flat of your trowel (almost like hammering a nail) in random locations, to create soft peaks resembling whipped egg whites. Then, ever so lightly, using long soft strokes, "knock down" and smooth out the tips of the peaks, to your taste. For a smoother, softer, subtler effect, apply a little less compound, use a lower angle on your trowel, and knock down more peaks. For a more rustic effect, apply more joint compound, use a higher trowel angle, and knock down fewer peaks. If you are working with a friend, make sure that you integrate both work areas, so the two different applications flow into each other. Make sure to step back periodically and look at your progress from across the room.

Be sure to remove the painter's tape before the joint compound dries, so the tape doesn't get stuck in the hard compound. At this point, you are ready to either paint, or paint and glaze, directly over the dried compound.

Difficulty Factor: Advanced
Time Factor: 2-4 Days
Materials and Supplies:
4"-12" trowels (2 or 3)
Drop cloths
Glaze (optional)
Joint compound (pre-mixed or powder)
Ladder
Paint
Painter's tape
Roller (thick nap)
Wallpaper scorer (optional)

TIP: Easy Touch-Ups

If an area of your wall is inadvertently chipped or nicked, the resulting white spot will be obvious. A fast and easy way to touch it up is to use paint and glaze that was previously stored in a Rubbermaid Paint Buddy, available at most home improvement centers.

IDEA: New Life for Outdated Wallpaper

Hand-troweling joint compound directly over old and outdated wallpaper can breathe new life into a stale room. In fact, we often do it because it eliminates the need to strip that old wallpaper! Remember to first score the wallpaper with a wallpaper scorer.

The plaster was hand-troweled not only on the walls of this kitchen, but on the ceiling as well. A rich ochre was used as the topcoat.

HAND TROWELING WITH TINTED JOINT COMPOUND

Another way to hand-trowel joint compound walls is to add color to the joint compound itself rather than painting over it. Since the compound is the wall color, nicks, dings, and picture holes don't require touch-ups. Color can be added to the compound in a variety of ways; we like to use universal tints available at most hardware or paint stores. You can also mix semi-gloss paint directly into the compound itself.

Mix the tint into the compound using a drill with an attachment that resembles an eggbeater; ask the person in the tool section of the local hardware store or home improvement center for the best size for your specific drill. Make sure that you mix in fairly large batches to keep the color consistent. Note the recipe you devised so it is easy to re-create it for the next batch; otherwise, you'll end up with different patches of color throughout the project. Now you can apply the tinted compound to the wall, using the process described on page 88. Once the application has dried, sit back and enjoy your new hand-troweled walls, or, as we like to do, finish it by rolling on a layer of a Ralph Lauren Aging Technique Glaze.

HAND TROWELING WITH PLASTER

Tinted plaster creates a more authentic European finish than either plain or tinted joint compound, because it has a finer, smoother, runnier texture. This also makes it much more difficult to apply. Because it's so difficult to apply, we have never attempted this technique ourselves. We recommend you hire professionals to do it; we have, and the results were amazing.

Above: The hand-troweled plaster walls give this guest bath a feeling of European elegance.

VENETIAN PLASTER

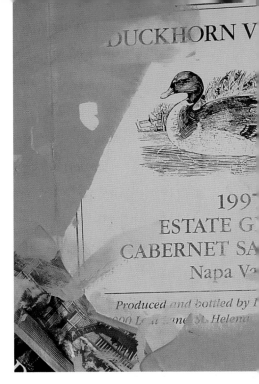

Think of an old world stucco finish, and that's what this new hand-troweled product creates. It has some special characteristics that differentiate it from joint compound. For one, depending on the manufacturer, it can have different additives: limestone, Carrara marble, or grains of sand, that, when sanded or burnished after the application, feature a marble-like or polished-stone finish. Venetian plaster requires a minimum of two coats, while plaster and joint compound require only one.

Venetian plaster can be found at specialty paint stores or at local home improvement centers. Behr has one of the most reasonably priced and readily available brands. It is sold in one-gallon cans just like paint, already pre-tinted, and comes in about 20 colors. Most Venetian plaster manufacturers stock a number of pre-mixed colors, but the store can also custom-mix any color you like.

Above (detail) and below: The walls in this wine bar were hand plastered using two different colors of Behr Venetian Plaster. The owners' favorite wine labels were applied to the wet plaster and then gently hand-troweled.

Do It: *Two-step Process for Venetian Plaster*

ach manufacturer recommends a slightly different process for applying their Venetian Plaster, so please read the manufacturer's instructions before you start.

As always, begin by making some practice boards; dry wall is the best surface on which to test. Practice your application techniques: holding the trowel, moving the plaster around, applying various pressures to the trowel and wall, and angling the length and shape of your strokes. Use these same techniques on your walls.

Difficulty Factor:
  Intermediate/Advanced
Time Factor: 2-4 Days
Materials and Supplies:
4"-12" trowels (2 or 3)
9" roller (thick nap)
Drop cloths
Hand polisher and sandpaper (optional)
Ladder
Painter's tape
Sample boards
Venetian Plaster
Venetian Plaster topcoat

Applying Venetian Plaster is minimally a two-step process: the first coat is rolled on using a thick-nap paint roller, covering about two-thirds of the wall surface in a random, yet even manner; the second coat is always applied with a trowel, covering the remaining one-third of the surface. For added depth and luster, trowel as many additional coats as you like; each additional layer will enhance the look. You can use different colors for each coat, though beginners should stick to one color, or two similar colors. Remember to keep each coat thin. Read the manufacturer's instructions for the appropriate time to add additional coats, as it varies widely from manufacturer to manufacturer.

After all your applications have dried, the next step is to sand or burnish the top layer by rubbing it, using a trowel or a hand polisher, and then to apply the manufacturer's suggested topcoat. Some manufacturers reverse this process—apply a topcoat first, then burnish or sand.

The ceiling in this living room received the same Venetian Plaster treatment as the walls. The large scale of the room offered the opportunity to create a number of conversation areas.

IDEA: Naked Plaster

Consider leaving the Venetian plaster as is, without any sanding or burnishing. It's a chunkier, less refined look, but one that might work for you.

IDEAS: Variations and Enhancements for Hand-troweled Walls:

- Add wine labels and slightly bury them.
- Add small stalks of torn wheat or dried flowers.
- Add any of your favorite photos or travel documents.
- Add a coat of glaze to age the effect.
- Add a coat of natural wax to enhance the look.
- Add a faux finish.

THE FABRIC WALL

Typically, most people think of fabric walls as those upholstered with traditional fabrics, such as chintz or damask, covered from floor to ceiling, or above or below a chair rail. Though fabric walls create a time-honored setting for a living room, dining room, entrance foyer, or study, we encourage the use of not only less traditional fabrics, but also more unique applications.

Right: Burlap, found in Hong Kong, was applied below the chair rail using wallpaper paste. The look softens an otherwise formal dining room and adds a unique touch. The wallpaper above the chair rail is by F. Schumacher & Co.

Design Diary:
Wall Fabric Sources

I am always exploring the streets and alleys of Hong Kong in search of new and interesting things. One day, while wandering around Sham Shui Po, an area known for fabrics, buttons, ribbons, trims, beads, etc., I found a wonderful burlap fabric with a plastic-coated backing. I wanted to call Anne immediately, but couldn't, since it was the middle of the night in the States, so I patiently waited until morning. We brainstormed and immediately came up with the perfect place to use it. We had a client (and now friend) who had tried her hand at a faux finish under her dining room chair rail. Although it looked pretty, it didn't do the Schumacher wallpaper and rest of the room justice. The burlap turned out to be the perfect solution. It gave the room a complementary twist on tradition, and reflected Nancy's personality.

Donna

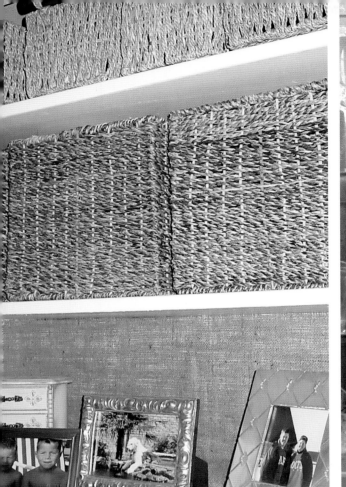

Above left and right: Burlap was used to line the back walls of these bathroom shelves and the butler's pantry.

FABRIC APPLIED LIKE WALLPAPER

Most often, fabric is applied in panels, which are installed over a layer of batting that has been stapled to the wall. The staples are then covered with a braided trim or gimp. This treatment adds visual depth and a layer of soundproofing, especially useful in today's media rooms. Although this is the most common method for applying fabric to walls, we have never personally attempted it, and would leave it to a professional.

Instead, we prefer to apply fabric directly to the wall, without batting or other padding, almost exactly like wallpaper. Wallpaper paste, spray adhesive, starch, and even staples are all effective ways to apply fabric directly to the wall. Which you use depends on the type of fabric, the weight of the fabric, and the weave of the fabric. We generally use fabric to cover parts of walls, such as below a chair rail, or just one focal wall. Considering our passion for natural products, it should come as no surprise that burlap is one of our fabrics of choice.

Manageable-sized fabric panels are an interesting way to apply fabric to the wall. The fabric is attached or upholstered, over batting, to plywood, acoustic ceiling tiles, foam board, or Homasote (a "green" product that is recycled and recyclable), using staples, hot glue, or duct tape. Use Velcro®, nails, decorative nail-heads, or finishing screws with a grommet to attach the panels to the walls.

It is really important to do your homework ahead of time—measure twice and cut once. You may even want to sketch the panel placement out on paper to make sure that your proportions are correct. If you plan to cover a wall entirely in 24-inch squares, you may find the room dimensions dictate that the squares be enlarged or reduced slightly to end up with even squares.

If you're using screws of any kind, make sure to pre-drill holes into the backing material, so as not to damage the fabric or jam the drill with the batting when installing the panels.

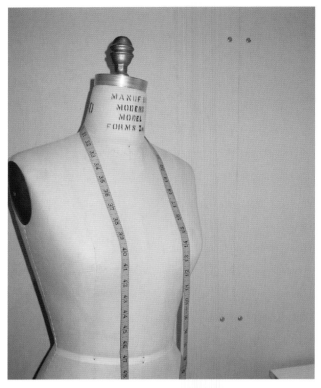

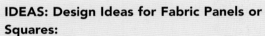

IDEAS: Design Ideas for Fabric Panels or Squares:

- Use upholstered fabric squares as a headboard.
- Use upholstered fabric squares to create a focal wall.
- Use fabric panels, the height of the wall, for a media room.
- Use fabric panels, the height of the wall, in a living room or dining room to display art.
- Try using natural textiles, such as linen, cotton, raffia, or burlap.

Above right and below right: Inexpensive linen from a theatrical supply company was used to dress the walls of the small office of a fashion designer. The linen was applied in panels and attached with decorative screws and grommets.
Opposite: Reed fencing was installed on the ceiling of this study for added color and texture; it provides a nice contrast to the decorative black beams.

COVERING WALLS WITH REEDS, BAMBOO, AND RATTAN

We also love to cover walls with reed fencing, bamboo, woven bamboo floor mats, or rattan panels. They add another layer of texture to the room, and bring in an organic element as well. And they work in casual, traditional, and even formal settings. But, you don't want to use them in a kitchen or full bath, as the moisture will cause warping and splitting. We select materials based on the following criteria: is it interesting, is it natural, is it unique, is it easy to install, are the texture and color right?

There are three critical factors for determining the total amount of material you'll need for your project—the pattern or design you'll create, the dimensions of the materials (for example, the length and circumference of the bamboo), and the total wall area to be covered. The pattern/design will be influenced by the product's length and width in relation to the wall area you're covering. Graph paper is an invaluable tool for sketching your ideas and calculating how much material you'll need. Your supplier can help you calculate how much you should buy. Just bring along your design sketches, graph paper, and the dimensions of the walls.

The installation process depends on the type of material you're installing; most are easily installed, directly onto the wall, using hot glue guns, staple guns, or finishing nails. Again, your supplier can advise you as to which works best with your specific material.

Above and detail opposite:
Bamboo floor matting was applied directly to the ceiling as a finishing touch to this Zen-like reading room.

Design Diary: Floor Covering for the Wall

Anne and I were shopping for shoes (a major addiction for us both) at Lane Crawford, Hong Kong's version of Saks Fifth Avenue. On our way to the ladies room, we both noticed a beautiful wall and realized that it was covered with tightly woven sisal, a natural kind of floor covering. It looked so gorgeous that we both vowed then and there to never look at floor coverings in only a traditional way again!

Donna

TIP: Bamboo Sources

Gardening catalogues provide lots of ideas and inspiration. The Internet is also a great source (for natural products see www.bamboofencer.com; they even offer bamboo poles that have been split lengthwise to make wall or ceiling installation much easier).

TIP: When in Doubt, Brush it Out

For installation on a wall or ceiling, always select reed fencing that has a polished finish, as polished reeds won't shed. If only unpolished reed is available, brush it down with a good sturdy broom or wire brush to loosen and shave off the loose fibers. Then give it a quick wipe and spray on clear satin polyurethane to seal it prior to installation.

TILE

Historically, the most common places to find tile in a home have been in kitchens, bathrooms, and as floors and accents in Mediterranean and Mexican style homes. Oven-fired clay tiles come in an array of shapes, sizes, colors, and finishes.

Today, tiles made out of new or unique materials are continually being introduced into the market, from stainless steel tiles to a concrete variety that resembles wooden floor planks. Some of our new favorites are small (about 1" x 1") glass and glass/metallic tiles, a bit expensive but high impact, and, mosaic tiles, which come in 12-inch-square sheets and resemble river pebbles or tumbled stones.

An easy and inexpensive way to add tile to a wall is to use it sparingly. Hang some decorative tiles every few inches over a doorway or around a window, or, create a tile chair rail midway up the wall. Tiles can be glued to the wall or hung using plate holders.

TIP: Stretch your dollars
Another way to save money on tiles is to cover most of the area with inexpensive tiles and mix a few more expensive tiles sporadically among them.

Above: Deep brown Italian porcelain tiles were used to sophisticated effect on the walls and floors of this contemporary master bathroom. White, green, and stainless steel are the perfect accents.

Right: The Ann Sacks metal tiles are set off by the 16-x16-inch red travertine backsplash and the Absolute Black granite countertops.

Mexican Talavera tiles can be used anywhere. They are the focal point of the nook created by the front staircase, right down to the baseboard.

BRICK

Brick walls have come into fashion again, partly because of the downtown loft renovations that feature exposed, original brick walls. However, when you see brick in newer kitchens, it is usually decorative brick facing. These facings are made from real brick, about ¼"–½" thick, complete with mortar, so it looks just like an actual brick wall.

Installing brick facing on your own is a complicated and time-consuming process that requires a fair amount of skill. We recommend you hire a professional; you'll save yourself a lot of time and frustration, and will almost certainly get a more professional result in the end, too.

We just love a brick focal wall—it can stand alone, or be used as a backdrop to highlight art or any other wall accessory. And, we both love the look of an antique brick wall that has been lightly whitewashed. This is a fairly easy technique. Simply paint the brick in a haphazard fashion with very watered down eggshell paint.

Right: Just inside the entrance foyer, the whitewashed two-story brick wall is home to a David Bates contemporary oil painting—the perfect spot for this spectacular piece of art.

Opposite: The whitewashed brick wall of the living room helps to define the space with a contrast of texture and color to the polished wood, warm tiles, and earth walls.

PANELING

Wall paneling is one of those things that often "comes with" an older home. Many people find paneling outdated and ugly, but we think it really depends on the style of the home. Friends of ours painstakingly restored the knotty pine paneling in their historic home back to its original state and their furnishings look beautiful in the "new" old surroundings.

If you want to remove your old paneling but are afraid of what you might find under it, then just paint over it! You'll need many coats of paint and you must first sand, clean, and prime the paneling, so plan on budgeting a fair amount of time.

A new twist for painting old paneling is to paint it in vertical stripes, using the grooves of the paneling as your guide. Choose as many colors as you like. If you are painting paneling with stripes in various widths, we recommend using more than two colors, as it will make the random stripes seem intentional, and give the room a more modern feel.

Opposite: The original knotty pine below the chair rail is set off by the deep red walls. Assorted flea market finds and mismatched chairs add to the dynamic nature of the room.

Right: The new homeowners spent several months stripping the old paint from the knotty pine paneling to restore the walls to their original beauty.

ROCK

Old homes and country cottages often feature rock quarried from the local land in retaining walls, foundations, fireplaces, and even walls and floors. Some homes are made entirely of local stone.

The color, finish, density, and shape of rocks vary from region to region, depending on what rock is a local natural resource. In the Hudson Valley of New York, bluestone abounds and its grayish-blue hues are evident in many homes, old and new. There's lots of sandstone and limestone in northern Indiana, and you'll find countless homes with that stone prominently featured in interiors and on exteriors. In eastern Pennsylvania, there are areas packed with older homes made mostly from local river rock and shale. And in Texas Hill County, there are many homes made of limestone or river rock.

Limestone color ranges from light gray to white and it is a soft enough stone to be easily cut into any shape or size desired. Conversely, river rock is dense and hard and very difficult to manipulate, so it must be used in the exact form it's found in nature.

Over the generations, most people have left the rock in their homes in its natural state. However, some homeowners have committed the mortal sin of painting the original rock! Once this is done, it's done; there is very little you can do to remove the paint, short of sandblasting. So, ignore the old chipping paint, select a new color of your choice, and repaint.

Some newer homes feature stone and rock, too. Though the initial costs can be prohibitive, the beauty and benefits are huge: no upkeep and the cost savings on heat and air conditioning are unbeatable. To save money, many builders are using stone veneers, which achieve the beautiful look, but forego the benefits, of real stone and rock.

Opposite: Anne's sister and her husband own a rock house in Texas Hill Country. The rock was left natural on the living/dining porch, which is used nearly year-round by the couple.

Above: In the main living area of the rock house, they painted the rock a rich red. They would have left the stone natural, but the previous homeowners had already painted the stone.

PART II: ACCESSORIZE IT

Art • Collections • More

The five individual square paintings, by artist Brant Williams, are viewed as one because the pattern flows from one painting into the next. The canvases can also be hung vertically. The paintings were commissioned to include the wall colors in this room as well as the adjoining rooms.

CHAPTER 4

ART

rt is subjective, a personal reflection that can make your house a truly unique home. Art has no functional purpose other than to bring beauty to a room. What one person likes, another may find distasteful, which is why we buy art based on what we love, not because it "goes" in a room or is a "good investment."

Location, placement, framing, and matting, as well as wall color, texture, and finish are all vital elements to creating the best impact possible for your art.

Opposite and above: The deep red contemporary oil painting looks stunning set against the various greens of the dining room. The walls are painted with Benjamin Moore Henderson Buff, the home-owners' taking off point for the room's color scheme. The sunflower painting is by Simon Burke.

WHAT IS ART?

So what exactly constitutes "art"? The answer is simple: art can be anything that dips into your imagination, touches you, and inspires thoughts or feelings. It can be an oil painting, an acrylic, a watercolor, or a mixed media. It can be a print, a lithograph, or a sketch. It can be a photograph, an antique map, or even a movie poster. Buy what you like and don't worry about matching your décor. Any piece of art that moves you in some way will find its proper place in your home.

SOURCES OF INSPIRATION

Inspiration for art can come from anywhere—even when you're not looking for it. It can be from a trip to a museum, a family vacation, the surroundings in your favorite restaurant, or even a piece of fabric. When you buy art for the sake of pure enjoyment, the theme or feeling is derived from your passions and what you love.

Opposite: A Vietnamese acrylic painting, almost 6 feet in height, was purchased for the stunning black and white color combination. The inspiration came from a piece of black-and-white toile fabric in the guest bedroom, which one enters just to the left of the painting. By hanging the art at the end of a long hallway, its dimensions are accentuated and it can be enjoyed by everyone on a daily basis.

Design Diary: Art Inspirations

Donna and I were shopping in Bangkok. We were exhausted and needed to take a break, so we stopped into the Holiday Inn Crowne Plaza coffee shop. As we walked in the door, there was a huge vintage poster of Grace Kelly and Taittinger champagne. I stopped dead in my tracks—it was absolutely gorgeous. I had seen it in magazines before, but seeing it in person overwhelmed me! I didn't buy one because I didn't have a good spot for it in my home, yet I couldn't stop thinking about it. A few years later, I found an original of the poster on eBay, and I just had to buy it, even though I had no idea where I would hang it. Once I had it framed, with a bit of trial and error, I found the right spot. To this day, it remains one of my favorite pieces of art and I will always find a special place for it no matter what!

Anne

Design Diary:
Finding the Right Art

I bought a gouache painting for my husband's 30th birthday. It was a close-up of a general's face, from a Chinese Opera, and I thought my husband would love it (not to mention that it was the perfect souvenir to bring home from Hong Kong). Anne's boys were very young the first time they saw the "General." Afterwards, she couldn't wait to tell me their reaction—they both wanted to know why I had Batman hanging on my living room wall! Ever since, I can't help but see Batman, and think of Max and Ben, every time I pass the painting. Art is truly subjective.

Donna

WHERE TO LOOK FOR ART

There are some obvious places to look for art, like shops and art galleries. Design magazines, books, Web sites, catalogs, movies, and TV shows are also great sources for ideas; they give you the chance to visit rooms and homes that would never otherwise cross your path.

There are less obvious places to search for art, too: try swap meets, flea markets, street fairs, yard sales, student art sales at local universities, or art fairs. Sometimes you can get amazing deals from these sources. Who knows, you may even purchase something that later becomes an investment piece!

Other sources may include art and photography magazines, photographers' and artists' Web sites, and even photographs that you already have. Consider taking your own snapshots to a photo shop and having them enlarged, or transferred into black and white or sepia. Remember, art doesn't have to be expensive to be valuable; it just has to mean something to you.

A master bedroom is personalized with a collection of photographs taken by a family member. The photographs were blown up, matted, and framed in a similar style, the larger photographs in more substantial frames than the smaller ones.

A room can be full of beautiful furnishings, yet still feel empty or incomplete, as though something you can't quite put your finger on is missing. Art is the instant fix to this problem. When you add a piece of art to a room, you gain much more than just the art itself—the art provides a sense of completeness, warmth, and beauty that personalizes and finishes the space.

Okay, so you know you need a piece or two of art to put the finishing touch on your room. How do you decide what to buy?

The Medium

Do you want a painting, a drawing, a photograph, or a poster? Your budget may direct this decision as much as your aesthetic preference. You may find an original painting you love, but just can't afford. However, if you identify the qualities you love about that piece, you can look for those same qualities in a print or a poster that suits your available funds.

The Mood

What sort of mood or environment do you want to create? Do you want the piece to evoke a serene feeling or be lively and stimulating? Is the piece thought provoking? Does it make a statement? Your existing furnishings and wall treatments can help point you in the right direction. A contemporary home decorated with off-white walls and sleek

Left: A painting of an oversized cup of hot chocolate, the homeowner's favorite warm drink, is perfect hanging above these leather ottomans in the kitchen nook.

Opposite: A framed portrait of the couple's daughter, Bella, leans above the mantle. The portrait is the work of artist m. Loys Raymer.

furniture would certainly be enhanced with a modern, abstract painting, but wouldn't really feel right with a traditional landscape. However, a traditional still life, framed and matted in a modern way, could look amazing in a modern setting. The same still life could work equally well in a traditional room when it's matted and framed in a more traditional way. That is the beautiful thing about art.

The Size

The size of the art can have a large impact on the mood and feel of the room. A large, single, dominant painting may be so powerful that additional art or accessories in the room would be superfluous, or even detract from the impact of the painting. A series of small, identically framed prints, however, can blend into a tableau created by the prints, a piece of furniture, and selected accessories.

The Subject

The subject of the art piece can serve as a design element in and of itself. Choosing your art based on subject is a good way to personalize your space, because it can reveal what's important to you, what inspires you, and even what moves you. A common, unifying subject can also allow you to combine various media (paintings, drawings, photos, prints, and decorative objects displayed together) and even art of different styles and from different eras. Let's say you love trains. You might take a vintage, sepia-toned train photograph and an art deco train poster and hang them side-by-side above a 1950s model train car displayed on a tabletop. As long as each piece has the same subject, you can make different styles and media work together.

The Color

Not only can the subject matter influence the feel of a room, so too can the colors in the art. Cool colors can contribute to a feeling of openess and relaxation, while bright and warmer colors can make a space seem more welcoming.

The Theme

If you find yourself with no clue about what kind of art to buy, another good starting point is to come up with a theme. Look around your daily life for themes that appeal to you. Maybe you like portraits, or botanicals; maps, or antique prints and posters; or dogs, or elephants. By choosing a theme, you'll always have something specific in mind when you visit galleries, walk a swap meet, or comb an art fair. And, you'll know that anything you fall in love with will work with your other art, because it has the same theme. As with a unifying subject, a unifying theme will allow you to combine art from different media, different styles, and different eras, and even art from different cultures.

Opposite top: The bright colors in this contemporary work of art make the entire room feel more inviting. The painting simply rests on the mantle above the neutral stone fireplace.

Opposite bottom: Hung above the bar area, a pair of simple wine bottle paintings looks right at home. The subject matter and style are just perfect for the home's contemporary interior.

Above: The red, brown, and beige color scheme of the bedroom is repeated in the vibrant piece of art hanging above the bed, which also acts as a headboard. The piece is a mixed media by artist Emmi Whitehorse.

QUALITIES TO LOOK FOR WHEN BUYING ART

If you are going to spend a substantial amount of money for a piece of art, there are a few things you'll want to consider. Make sure that the gallery will guarantee your purchase, that the art is what they represent it to be, and that they will refund your money if it's not. The same can be said for old posters and numbered prints—make sure that whoever you purchase them from is willing to stand by the sale.

Above: An original Jacques Lamy fresco style painting hangs on the focal wall of the dining room. It was purchased for its unique size and subject matter and it plays beautifully off the owner's blue-and-white Asian accessories.

Opposite top: A painting by artist Wendyll Brown covers nearly an entire wall of a home office in this Hong Kong flat. The size and style of the painting dictated leaving the piece unframed.

Opposite bottom: On closer inspection, this oil painting subtly reveals monks walking in the rain. Donna and her husband purchased the painting in Hanoi, Vietnam, and later had it framed in Hong Kong.

Ask a shop or gallery if you can take a piece of art out on approval before making the purchase, just as you might do for an area rug or other major purchase. Many times, they will agree to this if you leave your credit card information and consent to let them charge your card if they don't have the piece back within a certain time period.

TIP: Even You Can Own an "Andy Warhol"
Too bad we all can't march off to Sotheby's and bid on the latest Andy Warhol. But if you really love Warhol, there's a much less expensive way to get one. Check out www.allpopart.com for your very own Andy Warhol-esque portrait. Send them your artwork, choose a few options, and they'll take care of the rest.

APPRAISALS

You may also want to have the art appraised by an independent appraiser. They can tell you things like: market value, fair market value, marketable cash value, replacement value, loss in value, and insurance issues. Check your local art galleries for references, or you can research independent appraisers on the Internet. Also try the Appraisers Association of America, Inc., the oldest non-profit association of personal property appraisers. Do your own research on the Internet or at the library; check out what similar pieces by the artist have recently sold for.

FRAMING ART

The frame you select for your art is nearly as important as the art itself—it sets off the art so it can be viewed in the best possible fashion. The style, color and materials of the frame impact the look and feel of a piece immensely. Consider a nude oil painting. Framed in a simple, narrow black frame, it looks modern and contemporary. The same painting framed in a thick, ornate gold frame, would look much more classic and traditional.

SELECTING A FRAME

The selection of frames and moldings can be overwhelming, because there are so many choices. Framing materials vary from the ordinary to the extraordinary, from the more traditional wood, metal, and metal leafs to the more unusual bamboo, twigs, specialty mirror, colored plastic, clear acrylic, leather, etc., and range from stock moldings to intricately hand-carved frames.

Frame Size

Generally speaking, the larger the painting is, the larger (wider) the frame itself should be. A large traditional landscape is probably best suited in a wide, gold- or silver-leaf ornate-molding frame. A modern frame for the same painting would still be wide and thick, but this time sleek and simple. For a smaller piece, use a smaller and thinner frame whether the piece is traditional or not. These are general guidelines and shouldn't be followed religiously.

Frame Style

If you think about the mood you want to create and the mood of the art itself, it will help you narrow down the options and focus on specific frame styles before you even start. Do you want the painting to create a dramatic impact? Do you want the art to blend with other art or furnishings? Do you want the frame to create a statement of its own? The more intricate the art is, the less detailed your frame or molding should be; too much detail can detract from the art.

We always select a frame based on how it enhances the art, but a frame can also be a bridge between the art and the décor. If the surrounding décor in the room has gold tones or gold accessories, it would be natural to go with a gold frame. Some would favor the unpredictable choice and select a silver frame.

The salesperson at your framing shop is often an invaluable tool in making framing decisions. They usually have a well-trained eye, they really know the options in terms of materials, and they've had a lot of experience with virtually every type and size of art.

Opposite: An oil painting that was framed in a more contemporary style using a "floating" frame technique. The frame has an intentional gap left around the perimeter of the art.

Left: A simple yet substantial metallic frame was chosen for an oil painting purchased as a souvenir from Hanoi, Vietnam. The frame's color plays off the skin tones in the portrait .

IDEA: Falling in Love All Over Again
If you become bored with a piece of art, try changing the frame; you may be pleasantly surprised.

IDEA: Float Your Art
A contemporary way to frame a painting is with a floating frame: the art is mounted with a gap (blank air space) between the artwork and the frame which makes the art appear to float in mid-air inside the frame.

MATTING

Though not all art requires a mat (most original oil paintings are not matted, for example), matting is often a crucial part of properly presenting a framed image. It has an aesthetic purpose: it can highlight, contrast, or complement colors in the art; it increases the size, and therefore the impact, of the framed piece; and it can tie the art in with the frame and even the décor and colors in the room. Matting also has a practical purpose: it protects the art by raising the glass, so it does not touch, or abrade, the art. We favor very simple and clean mats in some type of off-white color. Having said that, there are occasions when we use colorful and even mismatched matting. In these cases, the matting becomes a distinct visual element in and of itself.

TIP: Matting Essentials
Always use acid-free matting, or museum-quality matting, to protect the art. Make sure you walk the art and matting into natural light before you buy it, so you can be sure of the true colors.

IDEA: Alternative Mat-erials
There are some unique alternatives to the standard acid-free matting you may want to consider: silk (we especially like raw or textured silk), burlap, corrugated cardboard, and numerous other specialty mats. Use these specialty mats selectively, as it is the art piece itself that you want to highlight, not the matting. To better protect your art, see if your framer can adhere the alternative material to an acid-free mat, so only the acid-free mat paper touches the art.

Above: The white matting and black frame help punch the yellow in the art which also echoed in the fresh forsythia.

Left: This quiet drawing, by artist Cuong of Vietnam, is matted with a weighted mat that is deeper on the bottom than on the top and two sides.

Below: Different matting was chosen to enhance each of these brightly colored Vietnamese paintings, yet all have the same simple black frame.

Double Matting

Double matting is when two or more mats, usually of contrasting colors, are layered on top of one another. The innermost mat is usually a very narrow line (¼-inch, or less) of color around the perimeter of the art. The color of the inside mat is almost always derived from the art itself. Pick a color from the art that you want to highlight, or, select a color that will contrast and make the image pop. (This can be especially effective with black-and-white, or, one- or two-color art.) The outside mat is placed on top of the inner mat, and it is much wider. (The width will depend on the size and style of the art and the frame.) We like the off-white family for outside mats because it is classic and clean.

Mat Size

A very common and safe mat width is 2½"-3" all around. This width works for 8x10 photographs as well as for a framed poster. A fresher, more contemporary look is to alter the size of the matting

GLASS

in some fairly dramatic way. Expanded matting increases the width of the matting all the way around and allows even a small piece of art to demand presence in a room. Another option is to increase just the bottom portion of the matting, which is known as weighted matting. A weighted mat is typically 2"-3" larger on the bottom than on the top and sides, but we sometimes like to emphasize the effect even more by making the bottom mat up to 6" wider.

There are several kinds of glass available for framed art. Non-glare glass eliminates the harsh reflection of light, but can take away from the crispness and color intensity of the art. Standard glass allows you to view the art with all its crispness and color, but it reflects light and can make the art difficult to see from certain angles. Both standard and non-glare glass can be found with a UV option, which protects the piece from fading, helping to preserve it. Be sure to ask your framer for all the options available.

DISPLAYING ART

Opposite: Matching frames and matting tie together a group of photographs by artist, mahesh brown.

Below left: The size of the Madonna and Child lithograph, entitled *Ave Maria St. I*, by Miguel Martinez, makes the image even more riveting.

Below right: A fresco painting, by artist Jacques Lamy, graces the staircase landing, allowing multiple viewpoints from which it can be enjoyed.

You want to place your art for maximum effect, so let's explore where and how to hang it. More often than not, you know you've got a blank wall or gaping hole that needs to be filled—behind a sofa, over a bed, or on a large wall. When you have a big space to fill, consider hanging a single, large-scale piece of art. Alternatively, a collection of pieces, arranged to act as one whole visual block, can create the same impact. Generally though, smaller spaces and nooks are better places to display smaller pieces. Follow your instincts; they're usually right.

IDEA: Need More Wall Space?
Easels are a nice way to display art even if you do have the wall space and they can be placed just about anywhere.

TIP: Art Doesn't Wear Sunglasses
Sunlight can damage art, so take great care not to place it on a wall where direct sunlight will fade and destroy it.

WHERE AND HOW TO HANG YOUR ART

For obvious reasons, larger art pieces are focal points, so they need to be on ample wall space, such as over a sofa, on a large wall in a dining room, in an entrance foyer, over a fireplace, or in a spot where your eyes are naturally drawn. Smaller pieces look better on smaller walls or in smaller spaces, such as in a bookcase, on a tabletop, on a small kitchen shelf, on an accent wall, or in a powder bath. When you hang small pieces, position them close to furniture or some part of the architecture so they don't appear to be floating in mid-air. Small art needs to relate to, and be anchored by, something else in the room. Groupings, or collections, another way to display art, are usually made up of smaller pieces arranged together and framed using similar or matching frames. (See more on collections beginning on page 132.)

Above: The art above the fireplace mantel is the work of Tami Rose. It was painted specially for the owners, incorporating many personal symbols.

Opposite: The Southern living room of a classical harpist. Note her daughters' portraits hung directly on the built-in wall unit.

POSITIONING ART

It has taken us years of practice to be able to hang art right the first time, and we are still learning and refining our technique. Here are a few of our simple, tried and tested "rules."

Don't Hang Your Art Too High

This is the most broken rule: Art should be hung at eye level, 60"-66" from the floor. Keep large art above a sofa to no more than 8"-10" above the back height of the sofa. We can't count the number of times we have seen art, that if lowered by a mere 6", would create a much bigger impact and make

the room feel balanced, proportioned, and, well, just right.

Different Heights for Different Locations

If the art is going to be placed in a dining room, try to lower it a bit more, keeping it at eye level from a seated position. On a stairway, place the art a bit below eye level, as the perspective changes as you go up and down the stairs. If you have two different-sized pieces hanging in close proximity, don't line them up at either the top or bottom, but rather, by the centers of each piece.

Right: The oil painting hangs as a focal point above a contemporary sofa that was custom made for the room.

Opposite: The light taupe walls in the dining room are the perfect background for the dynamic and colorful painting by Darren Vigil Gray. The wooden tabletop is a piece of old teak, which was buried for several hundred years in Indonesia. It took seven men to move it.

SOME OF OUR FAVORITE HANGING TIPS

- The color of the wall provides a great backdrop for displaying art. It can make a piece of art come to life. We don't advocate matching art and wall color, but sometimes an accent wall of matching color can make the art pop.

- Don't hang pictures alone! Get a friend or two to help you. Stand back and look at the art from across the room and compare opinions on placement prior to driving a nail into the wall.

- Mark the frame at the top, and measure down to where the wire stretches. This is where the hanger will go (not the top of the hanger, but where the hanger or hook actually cradles the wire.)

- Always put nails, screws, hooks, and hangers into the wall at an angle to make the hanger steadier and the art more secure.

- Lean art against the wall for a different look.

- If in doubt, hire a professional!

CHAPTER 5

COLLECTIONS

ollections can be important tools for dressing your naked walls. They can create as much dramatic impact as a single, dominant piece of art, and are a showcase for your own unique tastes, interests, and personality. They are great ways to tell stories. If you lack the funds or inclination to invest in an original piece of art, collections are a perfect decorating alternative—more often than not they are relatively inexpensive to put together. You may even already have all the ingredients for a wonderful collection right under your nose!

Opposite and above: A collection of Retablos—small oil paintings on wood of religious icons— grace the dramatic two-story entrance foyer of this Mediterranean home. Retablos' art has seen a resurgence in the past few years and continues as a major form of Mexican Folk Art.

WHAT MAKES A COLLECTION?

A collection is a gathering of like objects with common subjects, themes, design, materials, styles, or colors that, when grouped together, create a much greater visual impact than any single item would have on its own. While two of something is a pair, it takes at least three related pieces to comprise a collection. A piece of ironwork, an antique plate, or a piece of framed art can be beautiful on its own. But, if you group three antique plates, six small portraits, or ten ironwork finials in a single arrangement, the effect is more interesting and captivating.

TRADITIONAL APPROACHES

Perhaps the most common and traditional collection is a group of similar images framed and matted the same way: photographs, greeting cards, watercolors, charcoal sketches, textiles, antique maps, stock certificates, lithographs, or prints. But a group of like items, each framed differently, can also be presented as a collection, as long as they all share a subject or theme. Several antique botanical prints of different sizes and from different eras could each be matted and framed in gold frames of very different styles yet would still work as a collection because the common subject (the botanical prints) and the shared frame color (gold) tie everything together.

Right, above: A collection of hand-painted greeting cards were framed and matted. The actual cards measure just three inches square, but the matting and frames enhance their dimensions.

Right, below: A collection of blue-and-white plates, a gift from the homeowner's mother, is a classic accent on a small wall in this traditional dining room.

Opposite: This collection of family photos was put together by simply scavenging through the house. The various frames were intentionally left as found, showing how similar items, each framed differently, work beautifully as a collection.

Collections can also be created from unlike items tied together by a theme. A travel related collection might include outdated passports, British Air boarding tickets, photos of Buckingham Palace, and a London street map, all matted and framed alike. And your collections do not have to be limited to two-dimensional objects hung on a wall. Ceramics, ironwork, architectural pieces, vases, baskets, woodcarvings, plates, masks, trophies, and even souvenirs, can be grouped to create stunning collections. As long as shape, color, theme, or subject unify the objects, they will work as a collection.

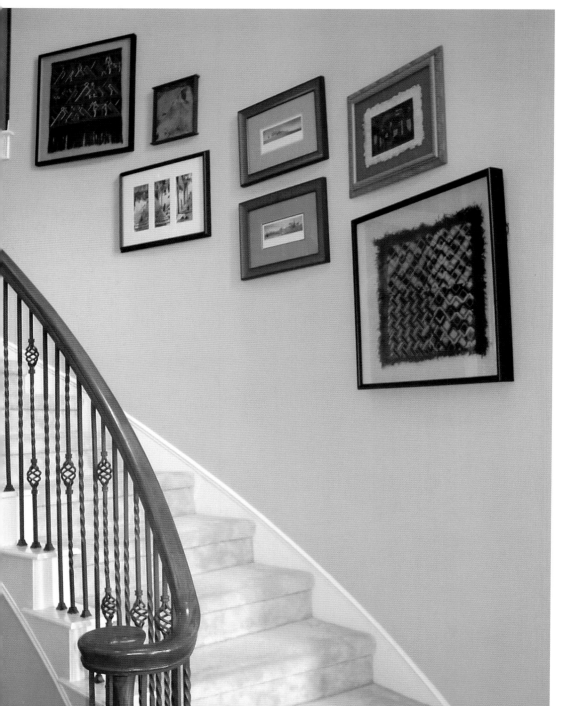

Left: An eclectic collection of art, acquired while traveling, is displayed along a winding staircase.

Opposite: Luke's bedroom displays his favorite collections of anything and everything baseball (and just a touch of football)!

Design Diary: Inspirations for Collections

I had been searching for some new art for a family room wall. When a good friend, Chris Salgado, sent us some of his digital photos of various New York City landmarks, it dawned on me that here was the art I had been searching for. I played around with them on my computer, edited them into 4½"x 4½" squares, and converted them from color to sepia. I used ready-made frames and matting from Aaron Brothers. The collection has a designer look and I didn't break the bank for new art!

Anne

A custom-built display shelf houses a collection of lunch boxes and thermoses.

GETTING STARTED

There are many different ways to start a collection. In fact, you may already have the components of a collection lying around your house—take a look at your tabletops, cabinets, attic, basement, and garage. Or, you can simply decide to start a collection based on your passions and interests. You can also "borrow" ideas for collections from books, magazines, and even other people's homes.

COME UP WITH A THEME

Many collections start out unintentionally. You may find that, over a period of time, you have accumulated a number of similar or like objects. Maybe it's a family tradition to see "The Nutcracker" every holiday season and you've saved the *Playbills* from each performance. For a great holiday decoration, just frame them in similar, inexpensive frames and mats and temporarily replace existing wall art with your very own "Nutcracker Collection." Another way to start a collection is to focus on something that you like or already have one of, and add to it, piece by piece, over time. Anne began collecting water pitchers years ago. After a while, everyone knew about Anne's water pitchers and newer pieces joined hers as birthday or holiday gifts. She displayed and redisplayed her water pitchers, first on small floating shelves, then, as the collection grew, in a built-in bookcase in the family room, and finally, with so many pieces, on top of the cabinets in her kitchen.

The homeowner had stored her mother's plates in a cabinet. They were forgotten for years until they were rescued and hung on the wall.

. . . .

TIP: Matching Not Required
If you have a collection you regularly add to, frame and mat the pieces in similar, but not identical, frames and mats, so when a new one is added, it won't matter if it matches perfectly or not.

. . . .

TIP: Gifts Made Simple
Collectors are easy people to give gifts to. When you start your collection, let your friends and family know and your collection will grow before your very eyes.

IDEA: Give a Gift that Keeps on Giving

For the birth of a new baby, put together a collection that can be treasured for a lifetime. Frame the front page of newspapers from the birth date, along with any items that are relevant at the time, such as advertisements from current blockbuster movies, the jacket from a current music CD, the local weather forecast, etc. You'll be creating a family keepsake.

Above: An ongoing collection of natural pigmented straw appliqué crosses from New Mexico is the owners' pride and joy. In fact, their 9-year-old son has started his very own collection to display above his bed.

Right: A collection of painted clay figures by artist Josefina Aguilar of Oaxaca, Mexico, cherished by collectors around the world, are displayed on the ledge leading into a dining room.

LET YOUR PASSIONS AND INTERESTS LEAD YOU

When starting a collection, think about the things that you love and that are important to you and run with them—you are not likely to lose interest in the things you love over time. There are many ways to turn your passions and interests into collections. If you love fishing, think about framing some favorites from *Field & Stream* and displaying them with a fishing reel, framed fishhooks, and some bobbers. If you're a sports enthusiast, try mixing your favorite covers of *Sports Illustrated* with some sports equipment (balls, hats, old bats or golf clubs, etc.). And if nature inspires you, how about featuring your favorite *National Geographic* images alongside some beautiful shells or rocks?

. . . .

TIP: Shop eBay

A good source for back issues of your favorite magazines is eBay. In fact, eBay is also a great source for vintage advertising and for music and movie posters.

SOURCES FOR COLLECTIONS

You may be surprised with what you already have wasting away in your attic or stored in the bottom of a sideboard that would make a great collection. China from various family members, mixed with your own, may look amazing displayed on a wall in the dining room. It doesn't matter if the china patterns and styles match; it's the family connections that tie it all together. If you're getting nowhere with the sources inside your home, start looking in other places. We often get inspiration and ideas from books, magazines, and even other people's homes. (Although imitation is the sincerest form of flattery, don't duplicate your friend's' idea; take the kernel of the idea and vary and personalize it with your own theme and pieces, to make it yours and not theirs.)

Design Diary: Inspired Sources for Collections

Anne's plate collection was too small for the kitchen wall that she had in mind and she had been searching for more plates to add to it when she instead found a different solution in a surprising source. While flipping through a Ballard Design catalog, she came upon a photo where 12-inch letters had been arranged on a wall like a monogram. Instead of buying new plates, she incorporated a 12-inch E, A, and T into the plate arrangement, which filled the space perfectly and created a unique focal wall.

Donna

Right: Our friend Wendy admired the way Anne displayed her plate collection so much that she asked Anne to help create a variation of it in her own kitchen. The mixture of plates, platters, tiles, and letters in various sizes and shapes works as a collection because all tie-in to the French Country theme of the kitchen.

Opposite: A framed collection of favorite decorating magazines take up nearly an entire wall in Anne's home office.

DISPLAYING COLLECTIONS

Just as there are numerous ways to create collections, there are also many ways to display them. They can be hung on a wall, leaned on a wall, or even arranged to flow from a piece of furniture and onto a wall.

DISCOVER WHAT WORKS IN YOUR HOME

The style of your home is an important factor in determining how to display your collections. You'll want to make sure the collection works with your furniture, rugs, accessories, and architectural style. If you have a very traditional home, consider displaying your antique teacups on traditionally designed wall shelves, or on cup hooks screwed into the shelf ledge. If your teacups are funky and your décor more retro, you could arrange them on various-sized, modern, clear acrylic boxes.

Left: The entrance foyer is the perfect location for a collection of colorful items. The pieces are displayed on chocolate stained wooden cubes that were purchased from the Exposures catalog.

Above: The owners' love of architectural elements is highlighted with dropped crown molding, window treatments, and the arrangement of the floral collection on the wall behind the bed in this decorative master bedroom.

TIP: A Great Source for Teacups and Plates

If you happen to be in New York City, check out Fishs Eddy for vintage and unusual plates and cups—we have been known to spend hours scouring through their inventory. If you don't have the opportunity to go to New York, you can check out their Web site at www.fishseddy.com.

Opposite: An extensive collection of colorful mini-prints by artist Kiki from San Cristibol, Mexico, ranging in size from 2"–10", make a lively presentation enveloping an entire wall.

Right: A collection of family photos leans against a shelf that was installed specifically to showcase the display.

"ONE-DIMENSIONAL" COLLECTIONS

A common way to display a collection is to hang it on the wall or display it on shelves. We call these types of collections one-dimensional. There are a few things to consider when hanging a one-dimensional collection.

Hanging Collections on a Focal Wall

When arranging a collection on a large focal wall, create the center area first and then work your way out. For horizontal displays, start with the center image and work your way out to the left, and then to the right. If the images are different sizes, line them up by the center of each piece, rather than by the tops or the bottoms of the frames. For a vertical displays, also begin in the center, then alternate pieces above and below the center item. Pieces should be grouped closely together, so the collection is viewed as a whole. Most people tend to hang items way too far apart, so place your items a bit closer together than you might think—for small items, about two-inches apart, for larger items, three-inches apart.

Collections on Shelves

Shelves are a very flexible way to display your collections. Items can be easily rearranged and changed as the collection grows and can also be effortlessly swapped out with changing seasons or when the mood strikes. There are so many shelving options available today. Floating shelves, a favorite of ours, have brackets built into the actual shelf, so they seem to float on the wall. There are also free-standing shelving units (with or without backs), which can stand against a wall, or be used as a room divider. Try industrial stainless steel shelving,

TIP: Shop for Shelves from Home
Catalogs such as Exposures, Hold Everything, Container Store, Ikea, and West Elm are great sources for shelving. Try out their Web sites at: www.exposuresonline.com, www.holdeverything.com, www.containerstore.com, www.ikea.com, and www.westelm.com.

normally used in a garage or a kitchen, in a living or dining room. And don't forget about the more traditional shelving approach—shelves supported by decorative wall brackets. When hanging more than one shelf on a wall, think about stacking them in a staggered fashion. It is a bit less predictable and can give a designer look to off-the-shelf items. Another idea is to place mirrors on the wall between the shelves, which adds depth and dimension to your collection.

Shadow Boxes and Collector's Boxes

Collections look great housed in a shadow box or collector's box. These are deep display boxes with glass fronts that can hold three-dimensional objects (sports memorabilia, souvenirs, old letters, maps, postcards, dried flowers, and antique textiles) and can be hung on a wall. A box for a die-hard Yankee fan could include a World Series program, ticket stubs, a collection of autographs, a baseball, a Yankee cap, Topps baseball cards, and some game-day or player photographs.

Above: An antique cabinet displays a collection of family pictures, instead of the usual china pieces. Notice how the collection expands from inside the cabinet, to the cabinet top, and onto the wall.

Right: A Japanese obi, a woven silk brocade sash, is draped over an antique Chinese ladder leaning on a living room wall. The Thai Buddha and Chinese ceramic bowl complete this unique Asian collection.

Facing page: A family's love of games and sports is unmistakably apparent the minute you walk into their game room.

"THREE-DIMENSIONAL" DISPLAYS

A more unusual way to present a collection is to use your furniture and accessories, in addition to the wall, as display components. We call this type of staging three-dimensional. It is less predictable because the collection flows from the wall to other surfaces in the room. A group of family photos can overflow from the wall into a cabinet or onto a tabletop. (Just make sure to hang the photographs very close to the cabinet or tabletop to make the arrangement seem obvious and intentional.) Three-dimensional displays can be a bit less obvious, too, and can include items from different media. Donna has an Asian collection which includes a Japanese obi, a Chinese antique ladder, a Thai Buddha, an offering bowl, and a Vietnamese oil painting.

Do It: *Hanging Collections*

Hanging collections can be a bit tricky and overwhelming. There are a few basic tips that can make the job much easier. First of all, measure the area on the wall where you will hang the collection. Then, reproduce that exact wall area on the floor—you may want to use newspaper and/or measuring tape to mark it off. Place the objects within the marked-off area, choosing one to serve as the starting or focal point (usually one of the largest pieces). Place the focal object near or in the center of the area, and, moving out from the center in all four directions, arrange the other pieces around it. Play with the arrangement until you are satisfied with it, keeping the pieces closer together rather than further apart.

Sketch the layout on paper and measure and record the places where each item will hang.

Transfer the placement markings to the appropriate place on the wall and then start placing your nails or screws where marked. Measure the back of each piece individually, because the hook or hanging wire will not be attached in the same place on each piece. And be sure to include the space between each element (right, left, above, and below) in your calculations.

Difficulty: Beginner
Time: 30-60 minutes
Materials and Supplies:
Chalk or #2 pencil
Hammer
Ladder (optional)
Level
Newspaper (optional)
Painter's or masking tape
Paper
Picture hangers
Tape measure, ruler, or
   yardstick

IDEAS AND TIPS: Hanging a Collection
• Wide matting brings the eye into the image that it frames.
• Grouping single pieces intensifies each piece.
• Consider a wall of empty frames.
• To make a collection read as one visual piece, keep the outside edges of the arrangement even.

A group of Sid Dickens' tiles, collected over a number of years, is showcased over the fireplace mantel in the family room.

CHAPTER 6

MORE IDEAS

*S*ome of our favorite walls are dressed with the most unexpected things—from masks, rugs, tapestries, quilts, and mirrors, to things you'd never expect could be hung on a wall, like doors, windows, old iron gates, fence panels, screens, and architectural pieces. Sometimes even things that might end up in the junk pile can create a dramatic impression on your wall after a new coat of paint or a simple cleaning. If you use your imagination, the possibilities are limitless.

Opposite: A beautiful Navajo Spider Woman blanket in the entrance to the master bedroom naturally draws the eye through the arch and into the next room.

Above: The whitewashed brick wall is an ideal location for a Chinese altar table, a beautifully framed antique Chinese flag, and tabletop accessories. The large swirls that look like tiny metal sculptures are actually antique Indian earrings.

THERE'S MORE THAN ONE WAY TO DRESS A WALL

Mirrors, masks, and even architectural pieces all make fabulous wall art. And often the best way to display textiles, such as tapestries, rugs, and quilts, is on a wall. We love the Asian influence and like to hang Chinese screens and Japanese fans. Other favorites include ethnic textiles, like African Kuba cloth, and antique French fabrics.

Opposite: The homeowners' collection of Retablos and small oil paintings of religious icons are displayed entirely across one wall in the great room. Note the old African Kuba cloth hanging on the wall.

Left: A Japanese fan from the late 1800's, purchased at Teresa Coleman's Fine Arts in Hong Kong, was framed and then hung above an antique Chinese lacquered cabinet.

Above: The unassuming beige walls really show off this extensive collection of art and antiquities. The round mirror juxtaposes beautifully with the lines and angles of the room.

ITIP: The Simpler the Better

When framing a mirror it's better to err on the side of the less ornate. This "less is more" approach results in a simple and classic mirror that is easy to move from room to room.

Above right: An old convex sunburst mirror is an ideal wall accent for a contemporary dining room.

MIRRORS

Mirrors can be found in just about any style imaginable, from traditional to contemporary, and everything in-between. Mirrors can be an affordable alternative to artwork, and are a beautiful way to expand and open up a room. They are available in many different finishes, from the standard, clear finish, to antiqued, bronzed, colored, and sandblasted, to name just a few. If you frame your mirror, keep the frame consistent with other frames and your overall decorating style.

TAPESTRIES

Tapestries have been made all over the world for centuries. Finer, hand-woven tapestries can be handed down from generation to generation, and with proper care can last for centuries. Medieval-style European tapestries are the most common and readily available, but some of our favorite tapestries come from more exotic locales. A Burmese kalaga uses a gold-thread embroidery technique that attaches sequins, velvet, wool, glass, and beads to re-create themes from everyday Burmese life and history. They are readily available in Thailand today. South African tapestries are made from mohair and feature thick textures and rich colors, often depicting Africa's best-loved animals. Tapestries can also be found in South America, frequently illustrating daily life in the Andes Mountains. Tapestries, like quilts and other textiles, are hung using rods. The rods, and decorative finials, can range from simple to ornate and are attached to the wall with wall brackets. Brackets, too, range from simple to ornate; just select brackets that match your rod.

Opposite: This ornate tapestry is all the art the pale yellow dining room walls need.

Above: A kalaga, a Thai beaded tapestry made primarily of glass beads and sequins, hangs above a traditional English sofa. It is equally at home in this Southern living room as it would be in a Southeast Asian room.

Right: An oversized traditional tapestry hanging in this two-story entrance foyer, gives the home a regal air.

Do It: *Creating Your Own Tapestry*

f you can't find a tapestry that will work for you, here's how you can make one of your own. You can do this as either a no-sew project using an iron and no-sew seam tape, or, as a very simple machine-sewing project.

For a traditional look, brocades work very well because they are lush and ornate, and are heavy enough to hang flat without curling up on the sides or bottom. Any other heavy, woven fabric, such as those with a pictorial scene (toiles) or large, repeated patterns work equally well. Consider a graphic geometric pattern like a bold stripe for a more contemporary look.

The wall space and the pattern/repeat of your fabric will establish the length and width of the finished tapestry. You will cut the fabric wider and longer than your finished piece to accommodate seams and hems. Cut the tapestry backing

Difficulty Factor: Beginner
Time Factor: 1–2 days
Materials and Supplies:
Bias binding (optional)
Brackets and screws
Decorative rod and finials (finials optional)
Drywall anchors, if needed for installing rod
Fabrics (tapestry, backing, tabs)—(optional)
Hammer
Interfacing (optional)
Iron
Ladder
Matching thread(s)
No-sew seam tape (optional)
Ribbon (grosgrain, satin, velvet or other—optional)
Screwdriver
Sewing machine
Tape measure
Trims (optional)
Tassels (optional)

fabric the same dimensions as the tapestry fabric. The backing fabric can be any compatible fabric. To determine the cut length, add 2" to the finished-length measurement (1" seam allowances at top and bottom). To avoid piecing and a distracting center seam, make the finished tapestry the same width as, or narrower than, the fabric.

At the top and bottom of tapestry and backing fabrics, fold edges in 1" toward the wrong side of fabric. Press. Stitch across tops and bottoms of each piece separately, ½" from folded edges. Lay tapestry fabric over backing fabric, with right sides of fabrics facing each other (like the tapestry is inside out). Stitch the two layers together at sides, ½"–1" from raw edges. Press seams flat; turn tapestry right-side out; press tapestry flat.

The tapestry will hang on a rod threaded through tabs at the tapestry's top edge. Cut tabs from fabric or a wide ribbon. Tabs will be placed 6" to 12" apart, depending on the weight of the fabric. For seam allowances, cut the tabs 2" longer than the finished length (anywhere from 2"-6"). Fold cut tabs in half. Insert about 1" of the raw edges of tabs between the top folded edges of tapestry and backing fabrics. Stitch over all layers to secure tabs in place. You can leave bottom edges as they are, or stitch them together. You can also add fringe, tassels, beads, or other embellishments, to your taste.

Note: A sew-in or fusible interfacing at the top and bottom will give the tab edge and hem greater stability, particularly with lighter-weight fabrics.

IDEA: Add a Border to Your Tapestry

You can also add a border around the tapestry, using either purchased binding or wide, fabric bias-binding you make yourself. Border widths should range from 2½" to 4". Cut tapestry and backing fabrics to finished width and length. Place tapestry fabric over backing fabrics so wrong sides of fabrics are facing each other. Stitch tapestry fabric to backing fabric around all four edges, about ⅝" from raw edges. Apply bias binding to all four edges of tapestry. Cut and fold tabs per instructions above and sew them to the back side of the tapestry.

If you can't find a tapestry you like, you can easily make your own. Here, a piece of fabric from the Alexa Hampton Collection by Kravet was trimmed in brown velvet and hung on the wall.

TEXTILES

Textiles come from all over the globe and reflect the uniqueness of each culture. They can be framed, hung like a tapestry, or draped over a decorative rod. Ikats are ethnic textiles that are tie-dyed and woven from cotton or silk threads; they are native to Indonesia, the Philippines, Japan, and even New Mexico. Kuba cloths are embroidered and appliquéd raffia cloths, hand made in Africa. Belgian lace, French Toile de Jouy, and handmade American quilts are beautiful wall textiles. Ethnic clothing can also make unique wall decorations. Consider a Japanese Obi or Kimono, an Indian Sari, a Navajo wearing blanket, or even Chinese shoes and hats.

Above: A piece of 19th-century French toile, picked up in an antique shop while on a tenth anniversary getaway, was framed and matted to create a unique work of art.

Opposite: A French-style needlepoint rug hangs above the headboard and extends nearly the full height of the guest bedroom, creating a dramatic piece of art.

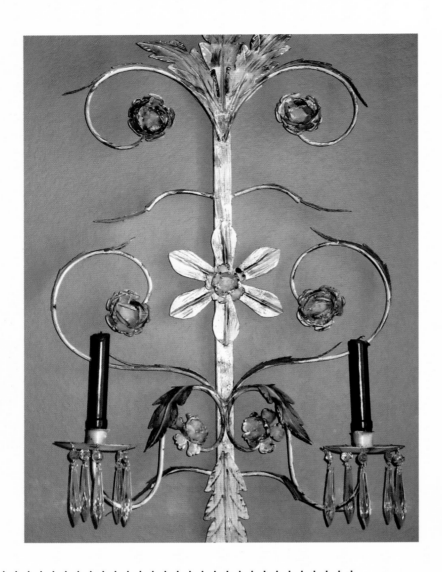

Above: An ornamental iron piece hangs on a faux painted brick wall, creating intriguing layers of texture and pattern.

Design Diary:
Turning Junk into Art

While rummaging through a warehouse sale, Anne and Wendy came upon a pair of painted iron wall sconces. I said, "They sure would be nice if they were a deeper color." And Anne said, "And they'd be even better with a few crystals, too!" We bought the pair, wiped them down using a brown oil-based gel stain, and drilled some holes to hang crystals purchased in the lighting department.

Donna

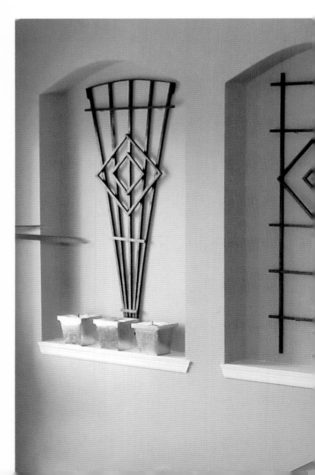

IRONWORK

Iron pieces, such as old iron gates and fence panels, window grates, garden trellises, and iron balustrade and railing accessories can make a great addition to a room, especially in old-world style homes. Whether displayed alone or grouped together, they add handmade craftsmanship to any room, and an element of depth to any wall. If you don't like the rustic look of rusted iron, you can remove the rust with a stiff metal-bristled brush and refresh the finish with spray paint. When Anne was on a tight decorating budget for a temporary living space in Hong Kong, she created an interesting focal point above the living room sofa with iron pieces of various sizes, shapes, and finishes. The result was inexpensive, unique, and quite impressive!

Right: Iron is a recurring theme throughout this modern kitchen.

Design Diary: Lightweight Alternative to Iron

My clients had three large niches high up in a great room and I had a hard time finding three affordable, large-scale pieces to fill them. I found the perfect iron garden trellises, but they were too heavy to get all the way up there. So Plan B was born—I went to the local home improvement center, purchased three wooden trellises, and spray-painted them in two different colors of "iron." They were extremely inexpensive, very lightweight, and to this day no one knows they're not ironwork!

Anne

This pair of old windows was found in an architectural "graveyard" with the old glass still intact.

ARCHITECTURAL PIECES

Architectural pieces can add a captivating effect to your home, too. Most large cities have at least one or two extensive architectural salvage or building-

material businesses that can be great sources of old and reclaimed architectural pieces (think about old doors or windows, antique columns, reclaimed wood for shelving or beams, railroad ties, medallions, floor grates, mantels, etc.) can be reinvented and used in new and unexpected ways. For example, hang a door horizontally instead of vertically, or hang several empty old frames on the wall for a new look, or lean them on a mantel or against a decorative shelf.

TIP: Look Beyond the Obvious
Landscaping or contractor supply catalogs are great sources for architectural wall pieces.

A gothic architectural piece decorates a living room wall.

SCREENS

Screens come in many shapes and sizes, from simple Chinese lattice patterns to those with intricate carving, inlaid mother-of-pearl, or stained glass. They can be as striking when displayed on a wall lik as they are standing on the floor. Japanese Shoji are made with rice papers which soften and diffuse light as it passes through them. We are very fond of the lacquer screen, typically three or four panels attached to each other with hinges, usually featuring painted Asian scenes or objects. We love screens made of fabric and leather. Fabric screens are readily available in stores and catalogs and are also easy to make yourself. Screens can also be made from more unusual materials, like iron, bamboo, or old doors. An easy do-it-yourself idea is to purchase hollow core doors and enhance them with paint, an aging technique, photos, or decoupage, connecting them using decorative hinges.

TIP: Uses for Chinese Screens and Windows
Donna loves to use antique Chinese wooden screens and windows as unique bedroom accessories, either as headboards, or in pairs flanking an upholstered headboard.

Opposite: Antique Chinese screens heighten the low contemporary leather headboard and add an unanticipated twist to this guest bedroom.

Below: An antique Chinese screen is used to soften the hard lines of a corner in this otherwise tranquil master bedroom.

Right: The fixed slatted wooden walls define separate areas within this contemporary home and, at the same time, keep the space airy, bright, and open.

Above: Framed Christening gowns once worn by Anissa's children have a special place in her home.

Below: A wedding invitation and birth announcements find a special place in a private back hallway.

SENTIMENTAL AND HEIRLOOM

Displaying sentimental items is also an interesting way to accessorize your walls. While wedding invitations and birth announcements are two fairly traditional options, Christening gowns and childhood garments are a little more unusual. A framed family tree can make a beautiful wall focal point; they always make for interesting conversation during cocktail parties.

Over the years, our clients have provided us with a fair sampling of odd and unexpected items that we have used as wall art. One of the most unusual was a rattlesnake skin, hung on a game room wall, which the client had actually shot and skinned himself. Not just the exotic, but mundane, everyday items, too, can become objects of attention with a little creative display. The possibilities are endless.

Above: An oversized coffee bag that once held coffee brought home from a Costa Rica vacation was framed in simple and graphic black. The coffee has long since been consumed, but the burlap bag serves as a unique souvenir and a daily reminder of a fabulous vacation.

Right: With its exuberant stack of pretty and colorful papers, the "gift wrap" room is one of Missy's favorite rooms in her home.

RESOURCES

ART

Mahesh Brown
214-321-2416
www.blackwhitebrown.net
Sid Dickens
www.siddickens.com

Jacques Lamy
214-747-7611
www.jacqueslamy.com

Michael Lyons
212-515-9369
www.michaellyonphoto.com

m. Loys Raymer
e-mail: mloys@hctc.net

Tami Rose
www.artbytami.com

www.allpopart.com

www.art.com

www.enjoyart.com

CATALOGS

Ballard Designs
800-536-7551
www.ballarddesigns.com

Container Store
888-266-8246
www.containerstore.com

Crate and Barrel
800-967-6696
www.crateandbarrel.com

Design Within Reach
800-944-2233
www.dwr.com

Exposures
800-572-5750
www.exposuresonline.com

Hold Everything
888-922-4117
www.holdeverything.com

Ikea
800-434-IKEA
www.ikea.com

Pottery Barn
888-779-5176
www.potterybarn.com

Restoration Hardware
800-910-9836
www.restorationhardware.com

West Elm
866-WESTELM (937-8356)
www.westelm.com

FABRICS

Robert Allen
800-333-3777
www.robertallendesign.com

Calico Corners
800-213-6366
www.calicocorners.com

Nina Campbell
www.ninacampbell.com

Designers Guild
www.designersguild.com

Donghia
www.donghia.com

Alexa Hampton for Kravet
800-648-5728
www.kravet.com

Andrew Martin
www.andrewmartin.co.uk

Jim Thompson
www.jimthompson.com

Pollack & Associates
212-627-7766
www.pollackassociates.com

FURNITURE

Baker
800-59-BAKER (592-2537)
www.kohlerinteriors.com

Bernhardt
www.bernhardt.com

Ligne Roset
214-742-2300
www.ligne-roset-usa.com

McGuire
800-662-4847
www.kohlerinteriors.com

Norwalk Furniture
419-744-3200
www.norwalkfurniture.com

Charles P. Rodgers
800-582-6229
www.charlesprogers.com

GENERAL

Home Depot
800-553-3199
www.homedepot.com

Home Expo
757-412-1299
www.homeexpo.com

Lowe's
800-445-6937
www.lowes.com

LIGHTING

Artemide Lighting
www.artemide.us

Flos
www.flos.com

PAINT

American Tradition Paint (by Valspar)
Available exclusively at Lowe's
800-445-6937
www.lowes.com

Behr
714-545-7101
www.behr.com

Benjamin Moore
866-497-9513
www.benjaminmoore.com

ICI Dulux
800-984-5444
www.iciduluxpaints.com

Kelly Moore
888-562-6567
www.kellymoore.com

Pittsburgh Paints
412-434-3131
www.ppg.com

Ralph Lauren
800-379-POLO
www.rlhome.polo.com

Sherwin-Williams
www.sherwin-williams.com

RETAIL

Aaron Brothers
888-FRAMING (372-6464)
www.aaronbrothers.com

Crate and Barrel
800-967-6696
www.crateandbarrel.com

Design Within Reach
800.944.2233
www.dwr.com

Home Goods
www.tjmaxxhomegoods.com

Ikea
800-434-IKEA (434-4532)
www.ikea.com

Pottery Barn
888-779-5176
www.potterybarn.com

Restoration Hardware
800-910-9836
www.restorationhardware.com

TJ Maxx
888-4TJ-MAXX (485-5299)
www.tjmaxxhomegoods.com

Z Gallerie
800-358-8288
www.zgallerie.com

WALLPAPER

Brunschwig & Fils
914-872-1100
www.brunschwig.com

Donghia
www.donghia.com

Innovations
800-227-8053
www.innovationsusa.com

Pierre Deux
888-743-7732
www.pierredeux.com

F. Schumacher & Co.
302-454-3200
www.fschumacher.com

Seabrook
800-238-9152
www.seabrookwallpaper.com

Stevens Paint and Wallpaper
Wallpaper and Wallpaper
  Installation
225-359-6542

Thibaut Wallpaper & Fabrics
800-223-0704
www.thibautdesign.com

VARIOUS/MISCELLANEOUS

Alpenglow Imaging: Digital
  photography editing
719-599-5391
www.alpenglowimaging.com

Amy Radford
Muralist
aboruff1@verizon.net

Ann Sacks: Tile
800-278-TILE (800-278-8453)
www.annsacks.com

Bamboo Fencer: Bamboo products
800-775-8641
www.bamboofencer.com

The Silk Loom: Silk fabrics
866-799-SILK (866-799-7455)
www.silkloom.com

Callaloo Company: Bamboo
  products
281-778-7681
www.my-callaloo.com

Define by Design: Faux Painting
  and Decorative Finishes
817-845-9558
www.definebydesign.com

Feizy Rugs: rugs and carpets
800-955-2669
www.feizy.com

Fishs Eddy: dinnerware, flatware,
  glassware
www.fishseddy.com

Merida Meridian: natural floor
  coverings, including seagrass
  and sisal
800-345-2200
www.meridameridian.com

Prua Hides: Hides and Hide
  Products
http://www.prua.us

Virginia's Drapery Workroom:
  Drapery
940-627-7185

MATERIALS AND SUPPLIES
GLOSSARY

Carbon paper: Any commercial carbon paper in any color; used to transfer art and design(s) directly onto a wall.

Chalk or #2 pencil: For marking guide points and lines.

Drop cloth: A purchased painter's drop cloth, old sheet, old shower curtain, or other large piece of cloth or plastic to protect floors and furniture while dressing walls.

Dry-wall anchors: Used to hang art (or anything heavy) onto a drywall where you need more strength than a simple picture hanger provides. We prefer the screw-in type: tap them into the wall with a hammer and then screw in the remaining length with a Philips head screwdriver.

Edger: A great tool for cutting in around doors, windows, baseboards, and trims without taping off. An edger is a painting pad (about the size of a chalkboard eraser) with a handle to make it easy to hold. Apply paint to the bottom of the pad and then drag it around the desired cut-in areas.

Hammer: Any kind of hammer that can drive a nail into a wall.

Ladder: Any ladder or household stepstool that reaches the height of your project.

Level: Both laser levels and traditional bubble-levels come in a variety of lengths. The 3-foot length is most flexible for most of our projects

No-sew seam tape: A web-like tape that is used to fuse two pieces of fabric together, using a hot iron. You'll find it in the notions department.

Paintbrushes: Be sure to buy good quality brushes for the best results. Use straight edge brushes for painting large areas and angled brushes for cutting-in around trims, windows, moldings, etc. Paintbrushes are clearly marked as to whether they are designed for latex or oil-based paints, stains, or glazes. Make sure the type of brush you use is compatible with your paint, stain, and glazes.

Paint trays and paint tray liners: Plastic, throwaway liners for you paint trays that make clean up easy, and allows you to use the same paint tray for different colors and glazes. Available where paint trays are sold.

Painter's markers: They look like magic markers, but dispense paint rather than ink. They are very useful for painting murals.

Painter's tape: For most projects, the wider the tape, the easier it is to use. We recommend you use at least a 2-inch width.

Painter's wipes: Look like baby diaper wipes and are an invaluable tool for cleaning up around doors, windows, baseboards, and trims, as well as wiping up drips and accidents.

Pastel Crayons: Resemble chalk wrapped in paper and create great shadow lines for limestone blocks.

Picture Hangers: Use whatever is appropriate for the size and weight of your art.

Plastic cups: Large or small drinking cups for mixing small amounts of paints and glazes.

Plastic or paper plates: To use as artist palates for further mixing of paints and glazes.

Pouncing brush: Looks like an old-time shaving brush or oversized blush applicator. It is essential for applying many faux finishes and glazes.

Primer: The first coat of paint on the wall, applied before (i.e., under) the actual wall color (topcoat). Primers neutralize the surface, covering colors and patterns already on the wall, as well as color variations and other post-prep imperfections. White is the most common primer color, but some topcoats require colored primers.

Putty knife: Most putty knives come in 1- to 3-inch blade sizes and are used for spackling, drywall repairs prior to paining, or wallpapering.

Rags: When used for faux painting applications, make sure they are white and lint-free. For clean up, any old rags will do the trick.

Rollers: Available in various widths from 4- to 18-inches. A 9-inch roller is standard and that's what we use for most of our projects. We like to use the 4-inch throwaway rollers on our faux painting projects. Nine-inch rollers also come in a variety of naps (the length of the material of the roller). Short naps are best for flat surfaces, and longer naps are best for rough surfaces, such as a hand-troweled wall.

Sandpaper: You'll need various degrees, or grades, of abrasiveness from coarse to medium to fine. When making repairs to drywall prior to painting or wallpapering, use various grades of sandpapers, starting with the coarsest first, moving all the way down to the finest.

Sample board: A 12" x 12", or larger, piece of foam board, illustration board, art board, or drywall sample on which to test paint colors, glazes, faux finishes, and techniques prior to applying to wall.0

Screwdrivers: Philips head and flat head.

Sea sponge: Available in various sizes, depending on your preference, they are necessary for applying various faux finishes.

Spackle: Ready-mixed compound for easy interior patching of plaster or drywall surfaces.

Spray bottle: Used for wetting down old wallpaper prior to removal. Any type of spray bottle will do, even an old glass cleaner spray bottle as long as it has been thoroughly cleaned.

Stirrers: Used to stir your paint, they are free with purchased paint. We always ask for a few extra stirrers, especially for faux paint finishes.

Tape measure: One of your most important tools. We recommend you use one that is at least 20 feet in length.

Throwaway paintbrushes: Inexpensive and available in both bristle and foam; both are excellent tools for faux painting projects.

Trowels: Straight- and angle-edge trowels, in varying widths from 4 to 12 inches. You'll use these to apply joint compound and plaster, and to burnish a Venetian plaster finish.

Wallpaper brush: Wide (6"-8"), flat brushes used to apply wallpaper paste.

Wallpaper paste: We like to use pre-mixed wallpaper paste that usually comes in one-gallon plastic containers.

Wallpaper scorer: A small, hand-held device with a pointed rotary blade (sort of like a pizza cutter or tracing wheel) which is used to lightly score wallpaper prior to either its removal or in preparation for another process, like brown bagging or hand troweling joint compound or plaster.

Watercolor pencils: They look like colored pencils. You draw with them directly on the wall, then go over your drawing with water using either a paintbrush or old white rag, making your pencil drawing look like a watercolor painting.

INDEX